EXCITED
and kind of
SCARED

Photos & Stories

CATHRYN WELLNER

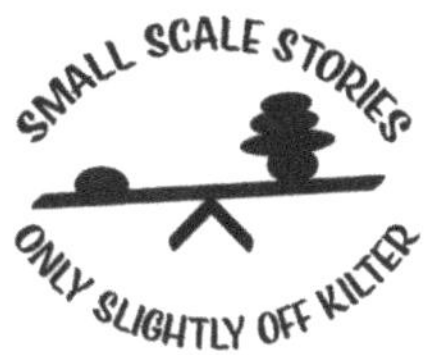

Small Scale Stories #8

Espoir Press

British Columbia 2018

Espoir Press
1002 - 1128 Sunset Drive
Kelowna, British Columbia
Canada V1Y 9W7

Excited and Kind of Scared (Small Scale Stories #8)

ISBN 978-1-988760-16-2

Fonts used are licensed through Design Cuts and include: Saltash, Sun Kissed, Ed's Market, and BW Surco

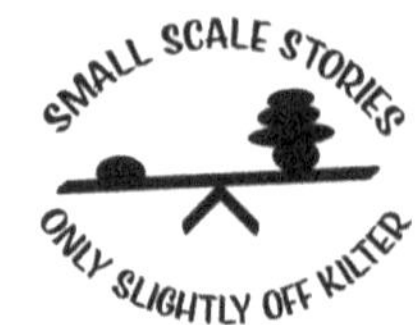

EXCITEMENT & FEAR

You stand on the precipice, staring at the chasm. Behind you is the life you have known. It is comfortable, but it no longer fits. Ahead of you is the Canyon of the Unknown. If you turn back, you will return to the familiar, the easy. It will not make you happy, but you already know how to move through the days it offers. If you step forward, off the edge, you will fly...or you will crash. What choice will you make?

The Small Scale Stories in this eighth entry into the series contains many of those moments of decision. The actors are leaves, birds, weeds, and building pipes. They are metaphors. You will understand their excitement and their fear.

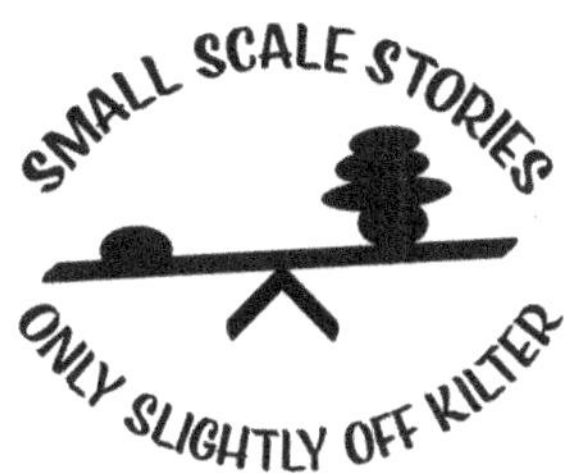

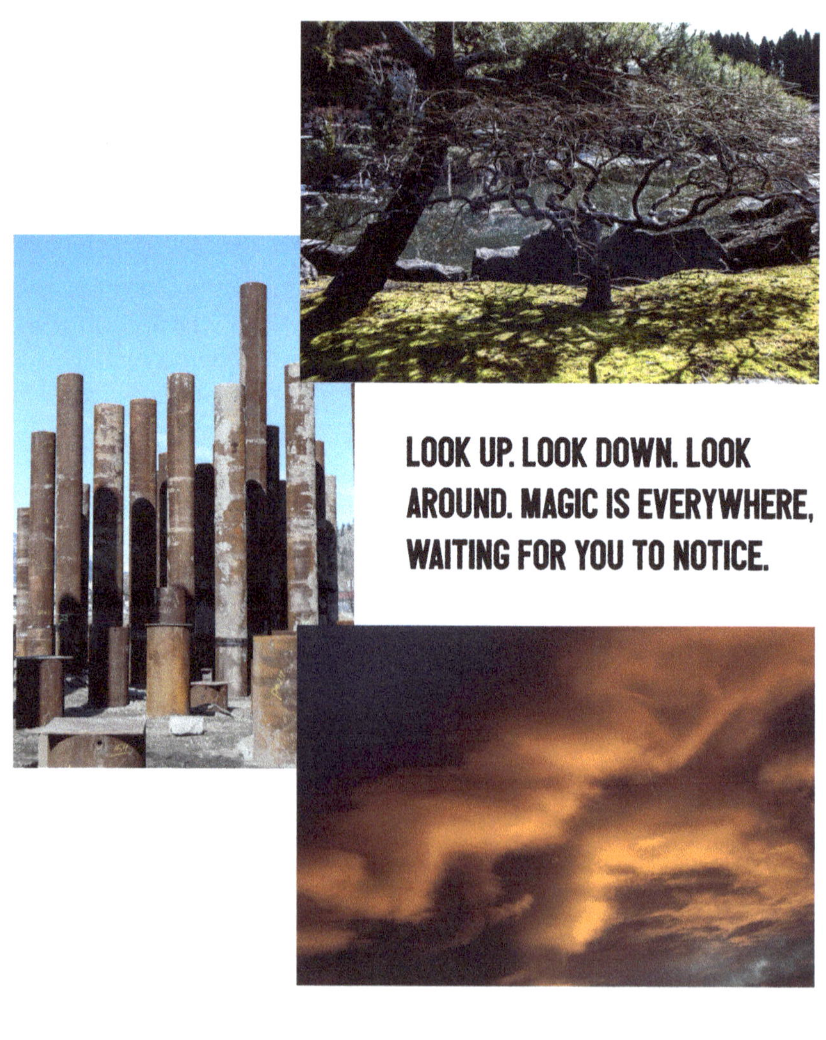
LOOK UP. LOOK DOWN. LOOK AROUND. MAGIC IS EVERYWHERE, WAITING FOR YOU TO NOTICE.

If you have ever been afraid...
If you have ever been excited...

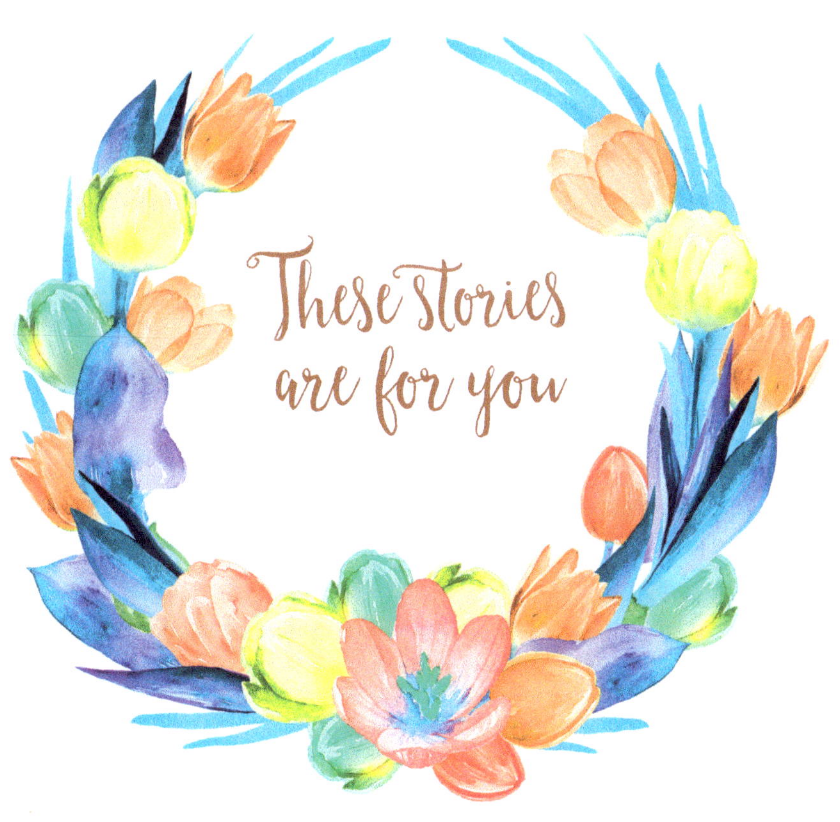

THE STORIES

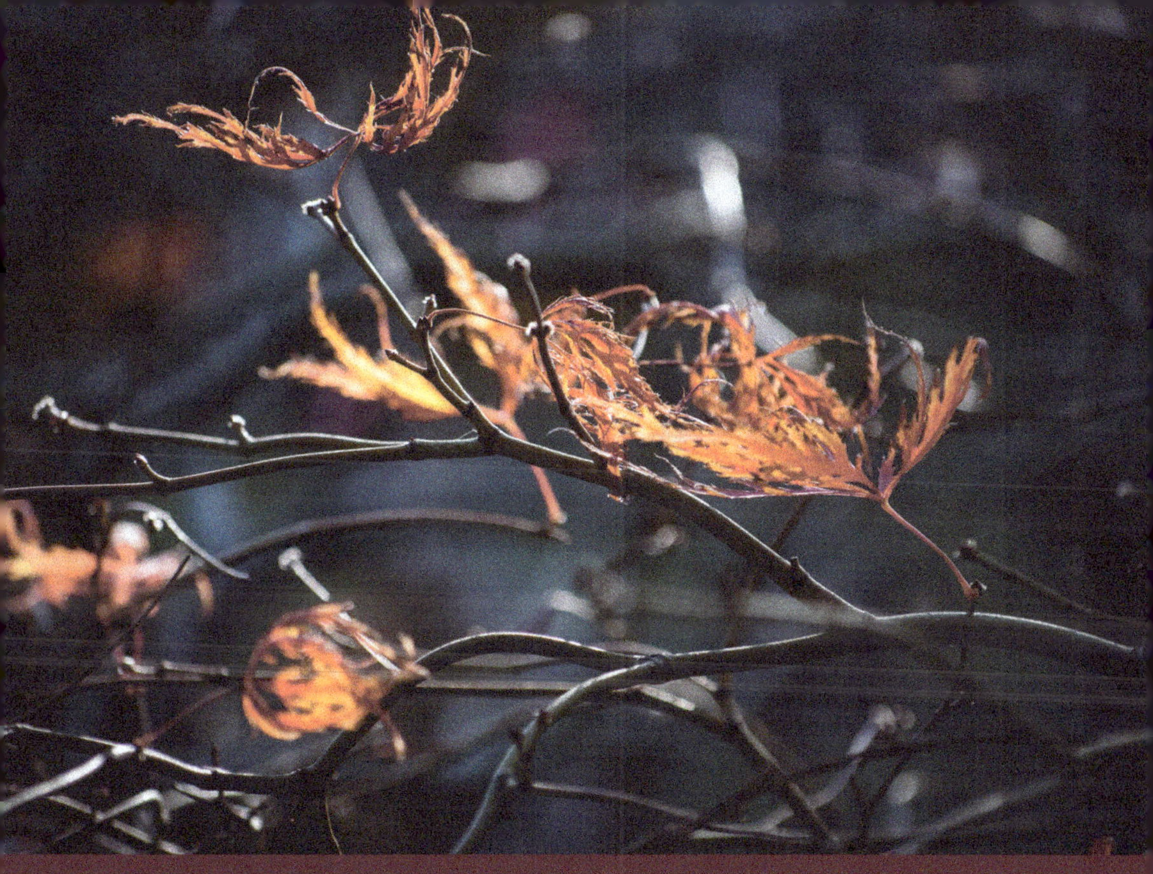

Before long they would leave Tree, the only home they knew. They were excited and kind of scared. They had dreamed of this moment. Now that it was close, they wanted to put it off as long as possible.

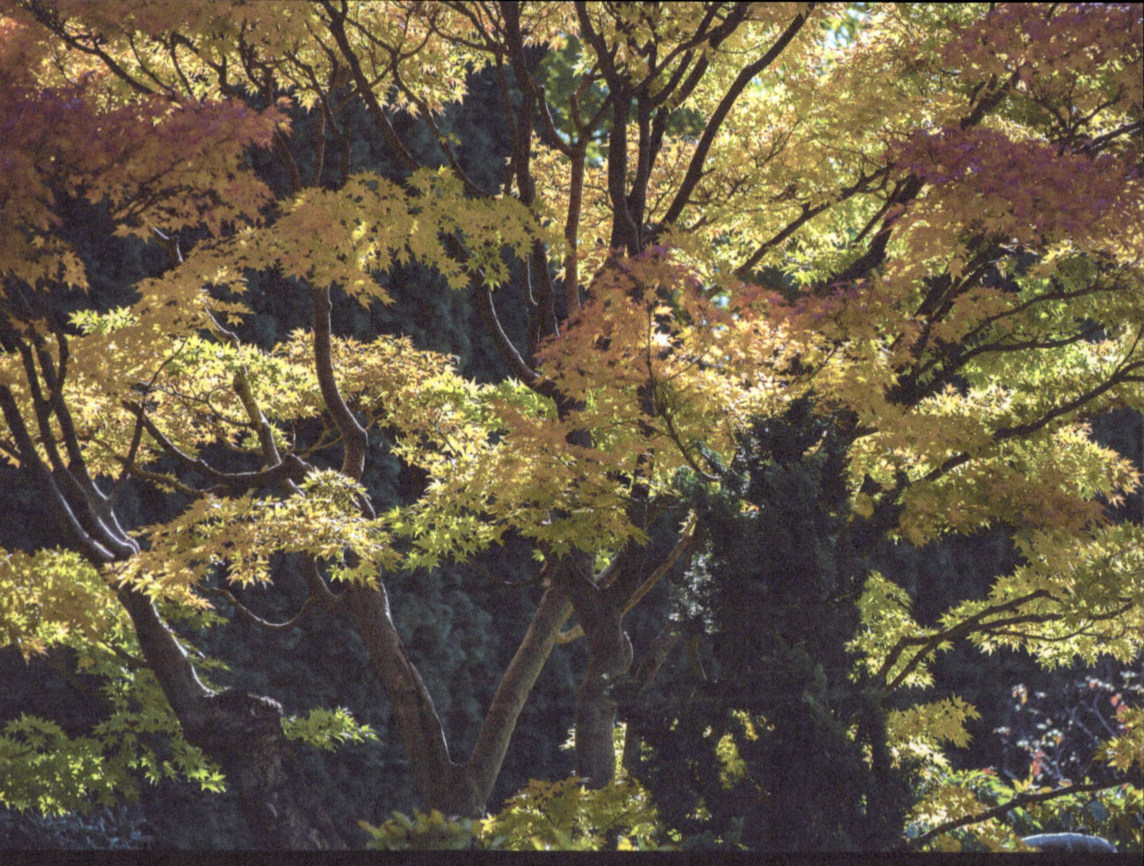

During days of grey clouds and rain, Leaves wondered if they would miss this year's Glory Time. Then Sun reappeared, and they shone like gold from first light to day's darkness.

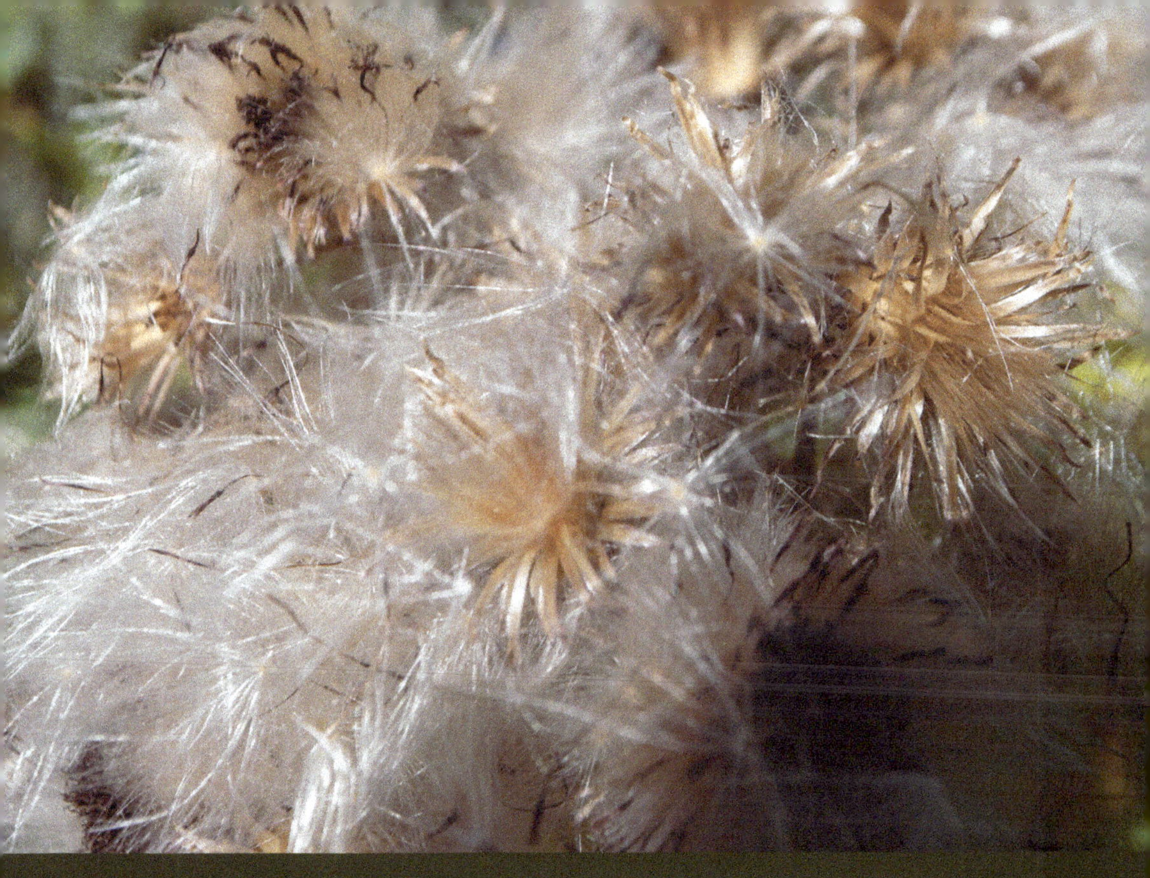

Their bright yellows faded and dried. What replaced them was even more glorious and glossy. They laughed and told stories, knowing Wind would soon scatter them far and wide, to begin new families.

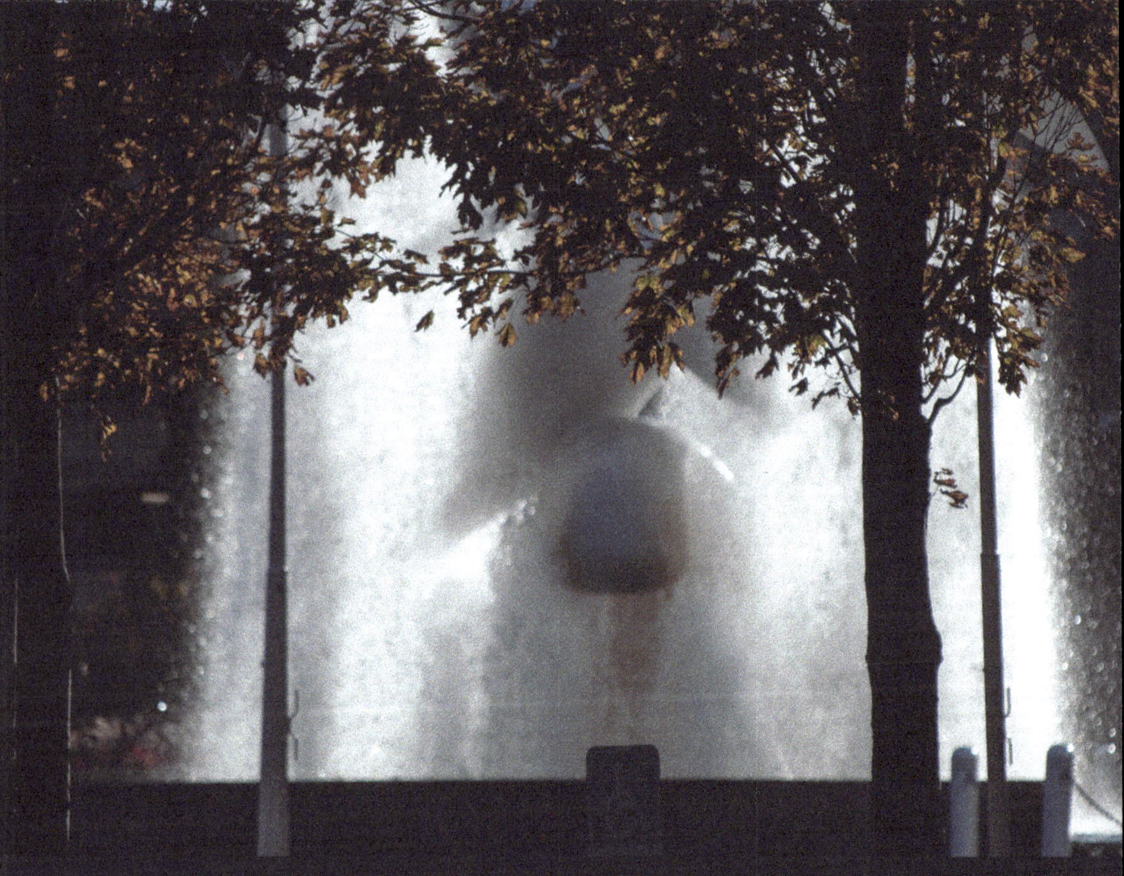

Fountain and trees were preparing for Hallowe'en. They practiced spooky looks with the help of Sun. They were not sure if they could carry it off once Sun disappeared for the night and hoped children would start trick or treating early.

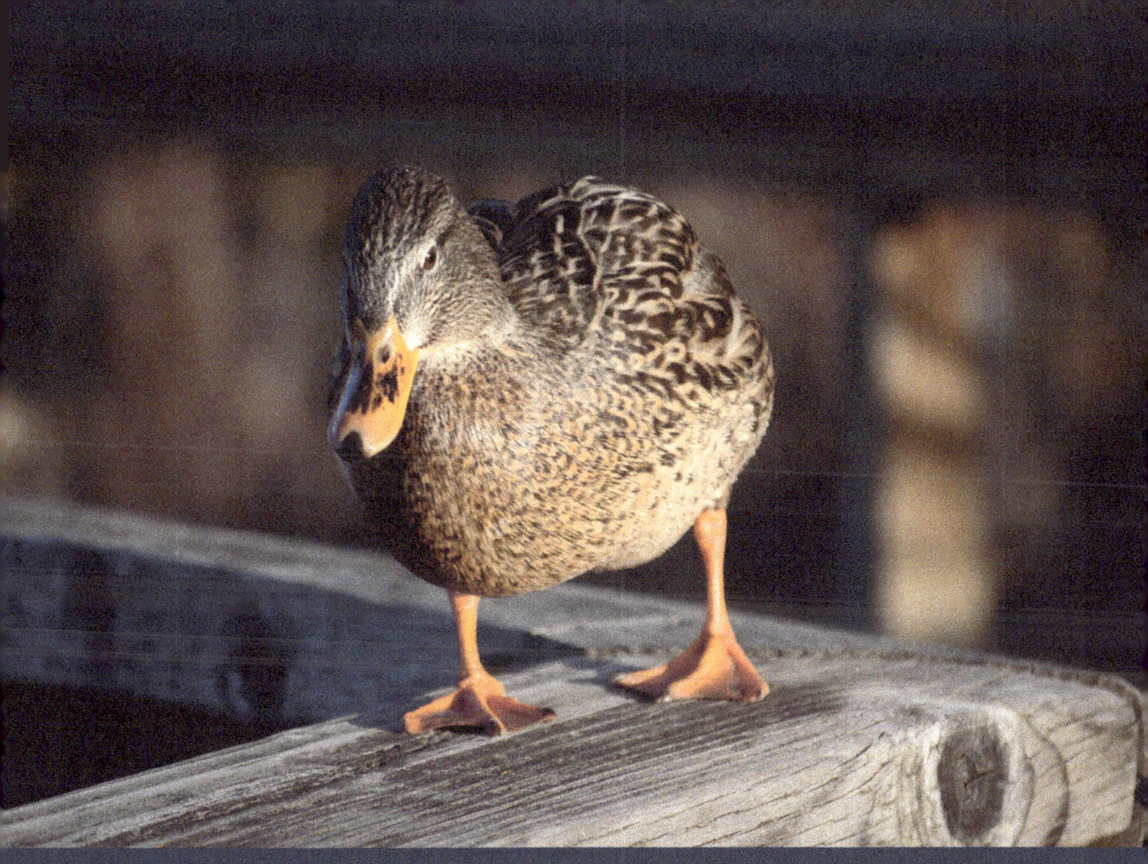

She was trying out her stealth walk. Cool, quiet, and unobtrusive was her goal. If she sneaked up on Seed Bringer before the human brought out her seeds, she could eat lots of them before the other ducks knew what was happening.

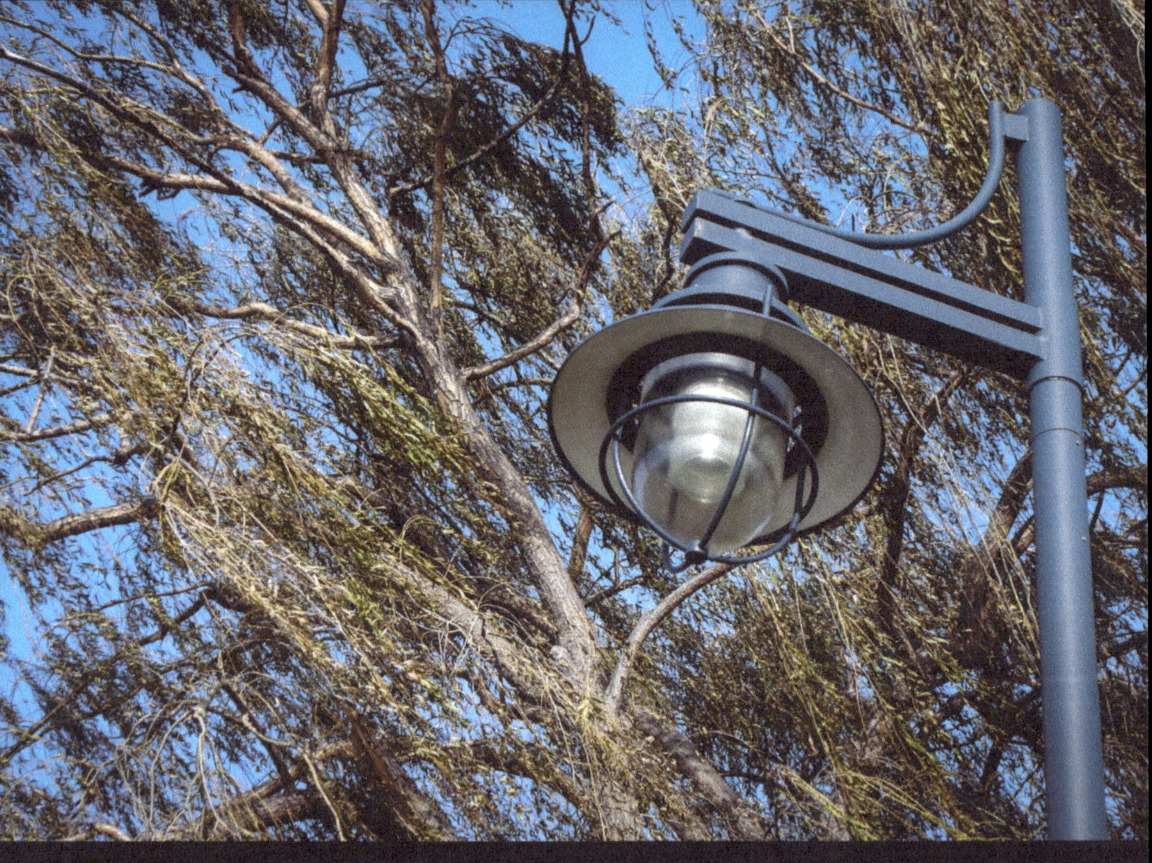

Willow overheard people talk about a book, *Who Has Seen the Wind.* He wondered how anyone walking by him today could NOT have seen the wind. Lamp post swayed in agreement.

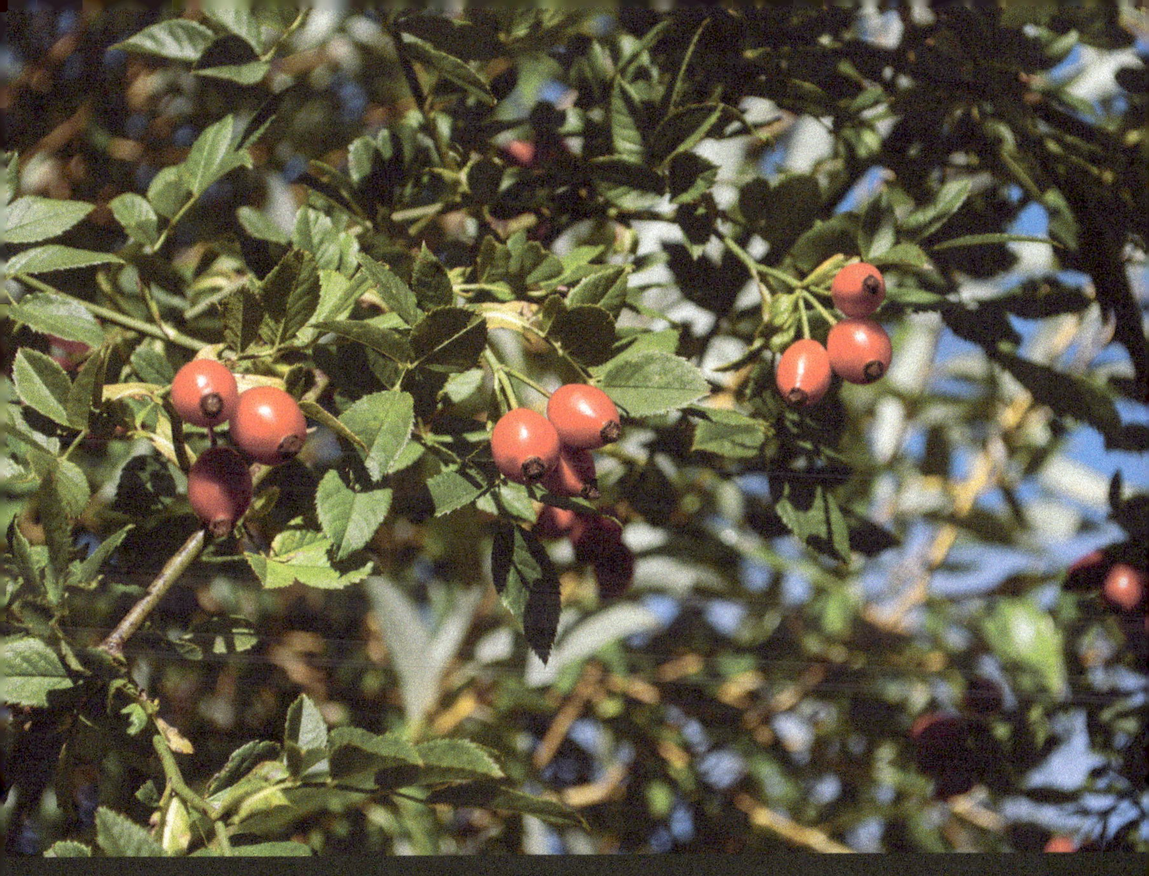

Rose Bush was pleased. It had been a good summer for triplets. She had enjoyed the admiration of passersby. Now her offspring were maturing into stunning rose hips. The birds they attracted would keep her company in the Growing-Dark time.

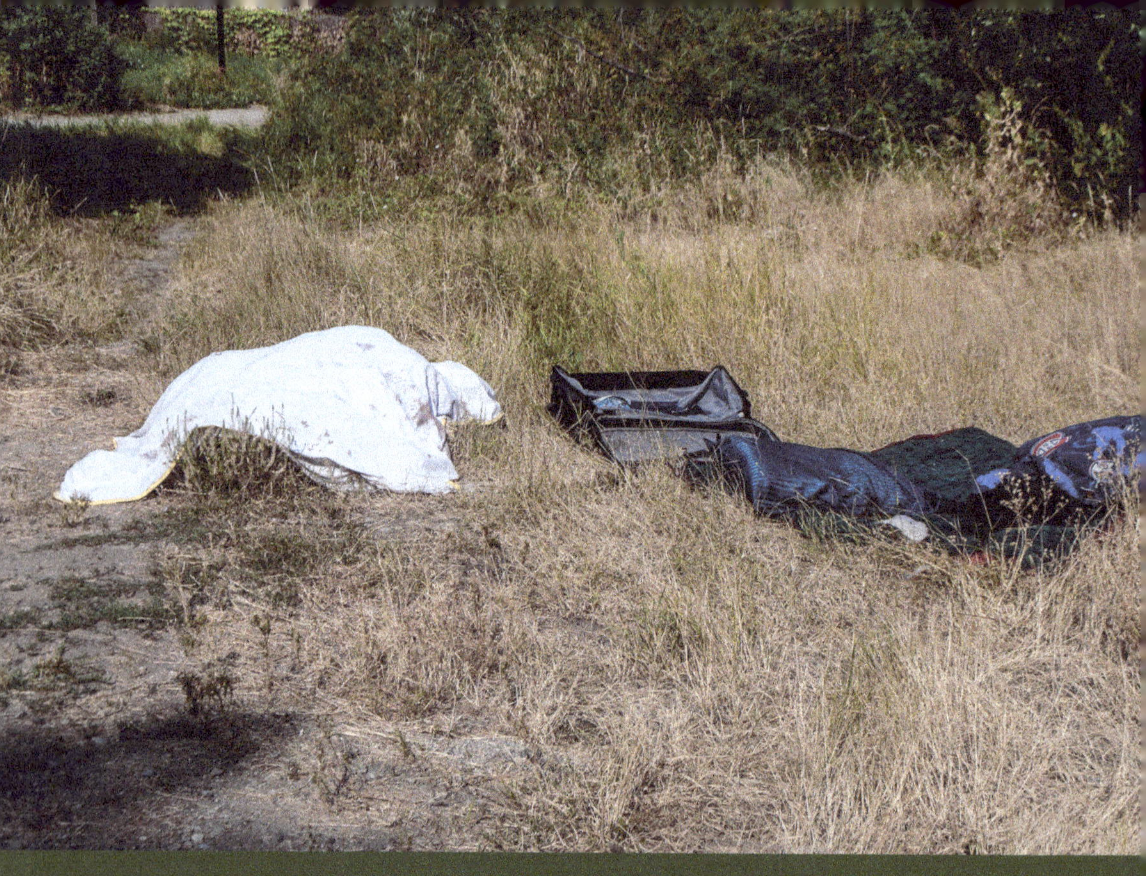

Tarp loved Sun's warmth. Suitcase was happy to be free of smelly socks. Sleeping bags were airing out the odors of unwashed bodies. For a while they were happy to lie on the grass. Then they began to worry about the lost souls who left them there.

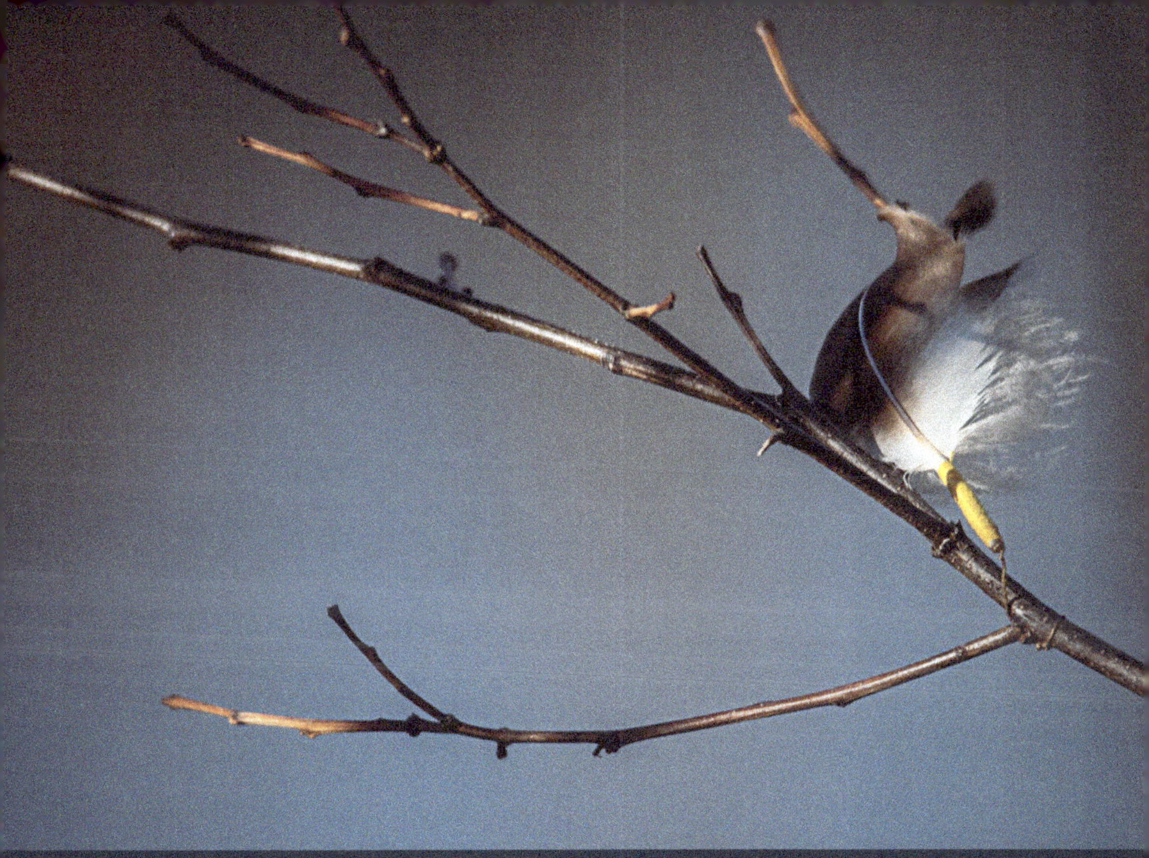

Eagle Feather never imagined he would end up tied to a branch, but he was happy with his fate. He had been chosen by a grieving man, to represent the spirit of his brother, whose death had come much too early.

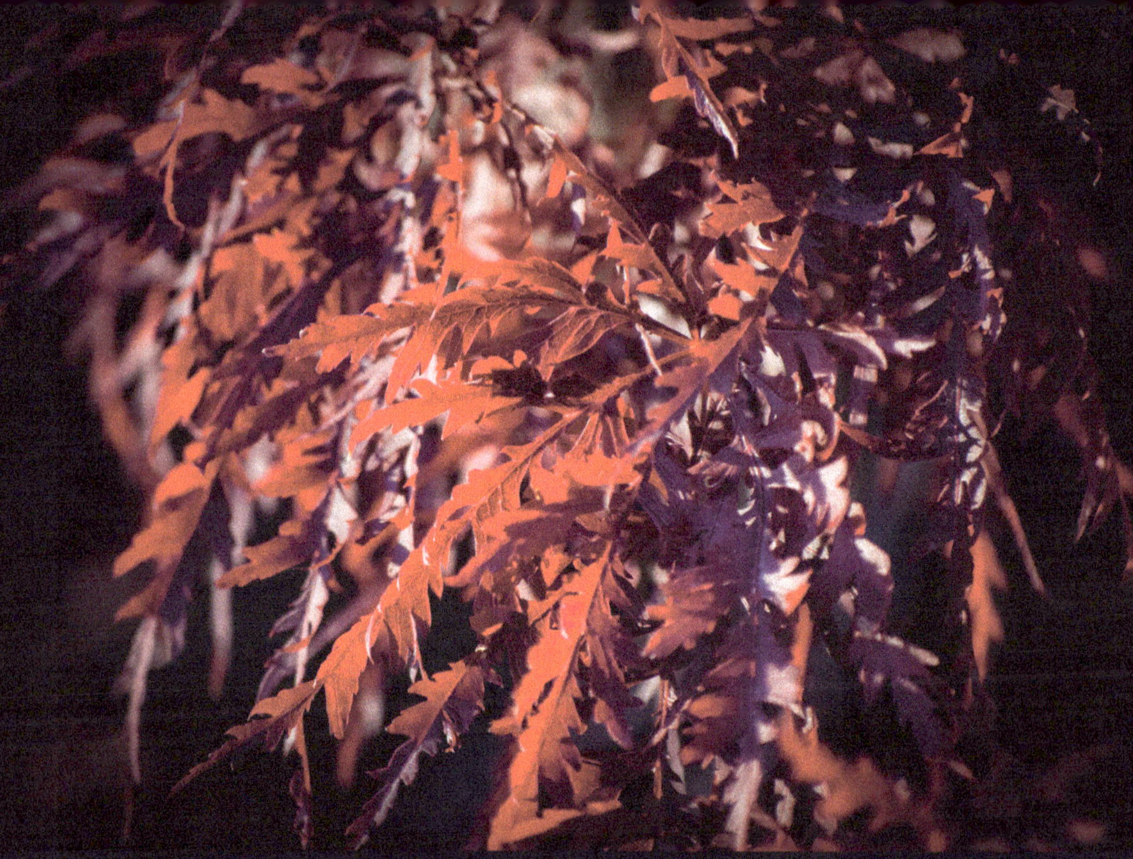

Leaves knew they would soon fall from their branches. They were swapping stories, reminiscing about summer's good old days. Their reveries shifted direction when someone remembered the farter who walked by every day. They laughed so hard some of them fell early.

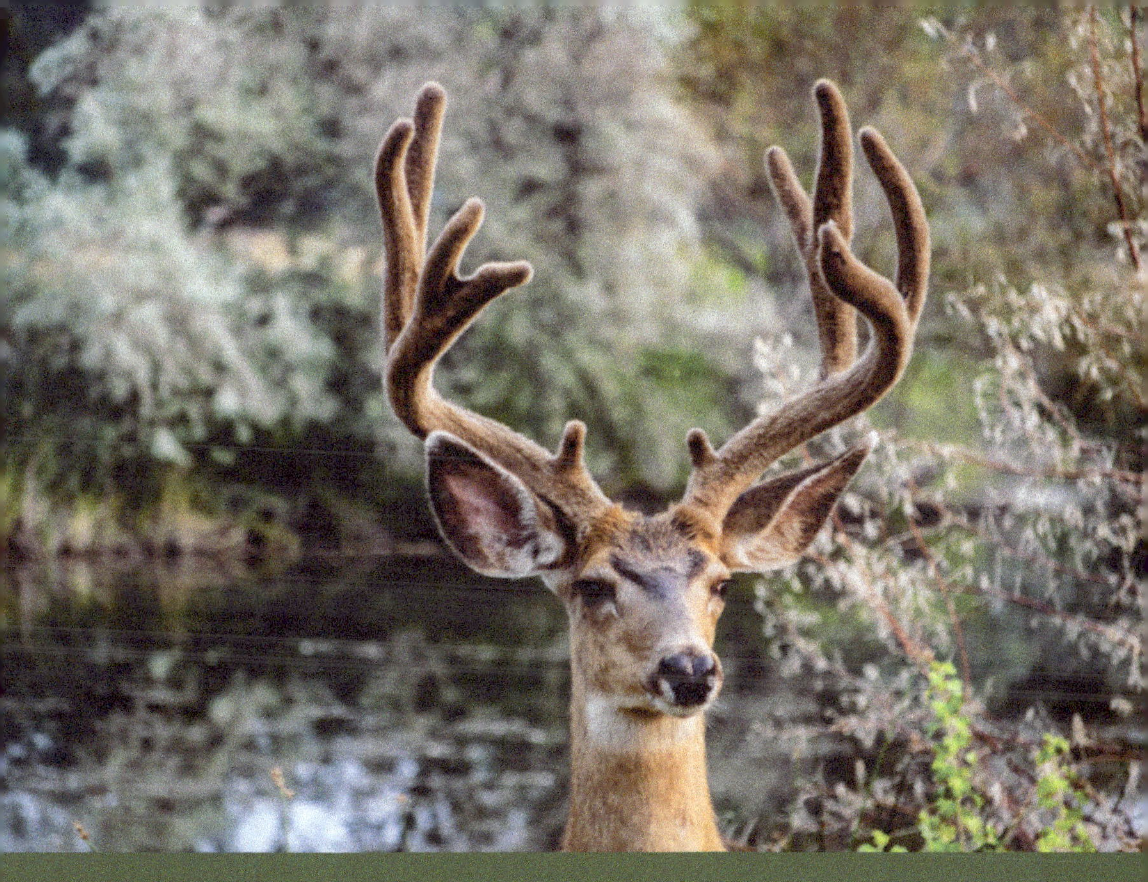

As his antlers grew, Buck dreamed of the does he would woo and the rivals he would fight for their love. Mostly the dreams were delicious, but some days he longed for a doe who would not expect him to fight for her.

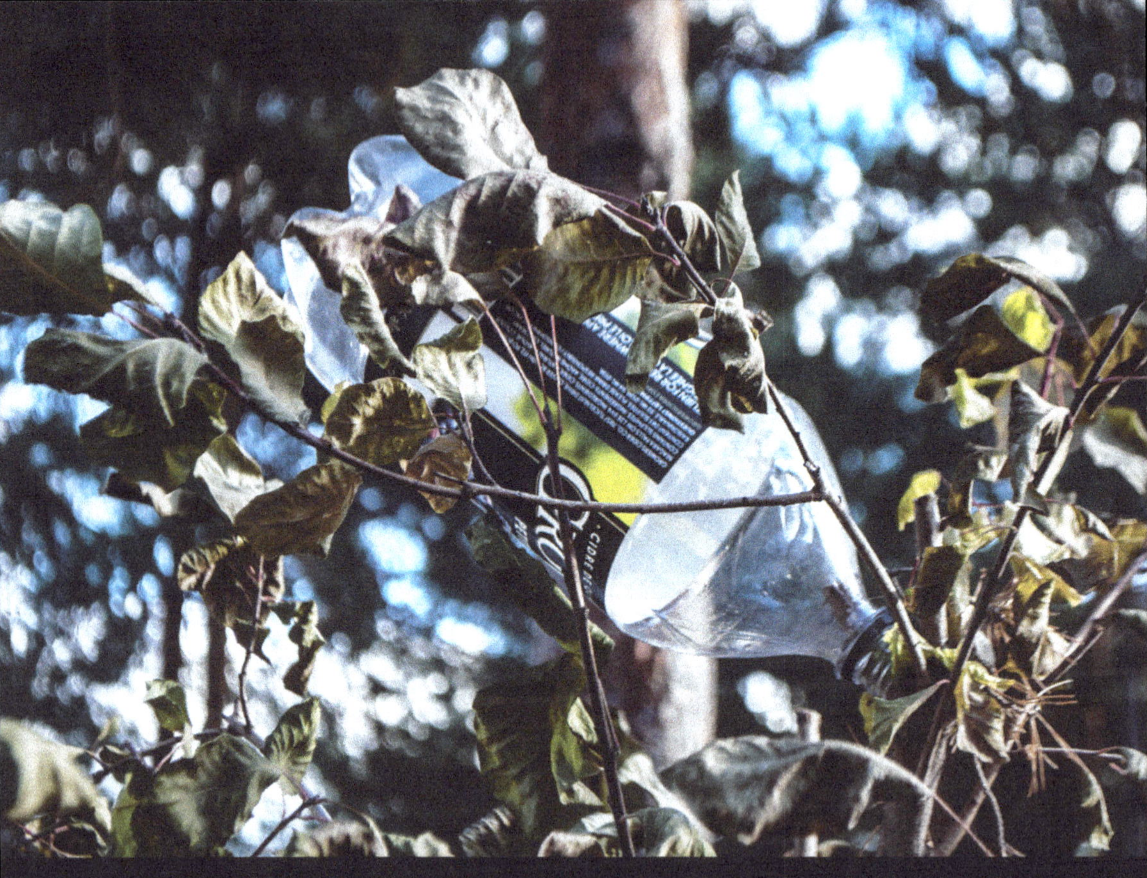

Bottle had done his job well, keeping the liquid inside him safe. But once the humans drained him, they humiliated him by sticking him on a limb and abandoning him. He would show them. He would retain his shape long after they had lost theirs.

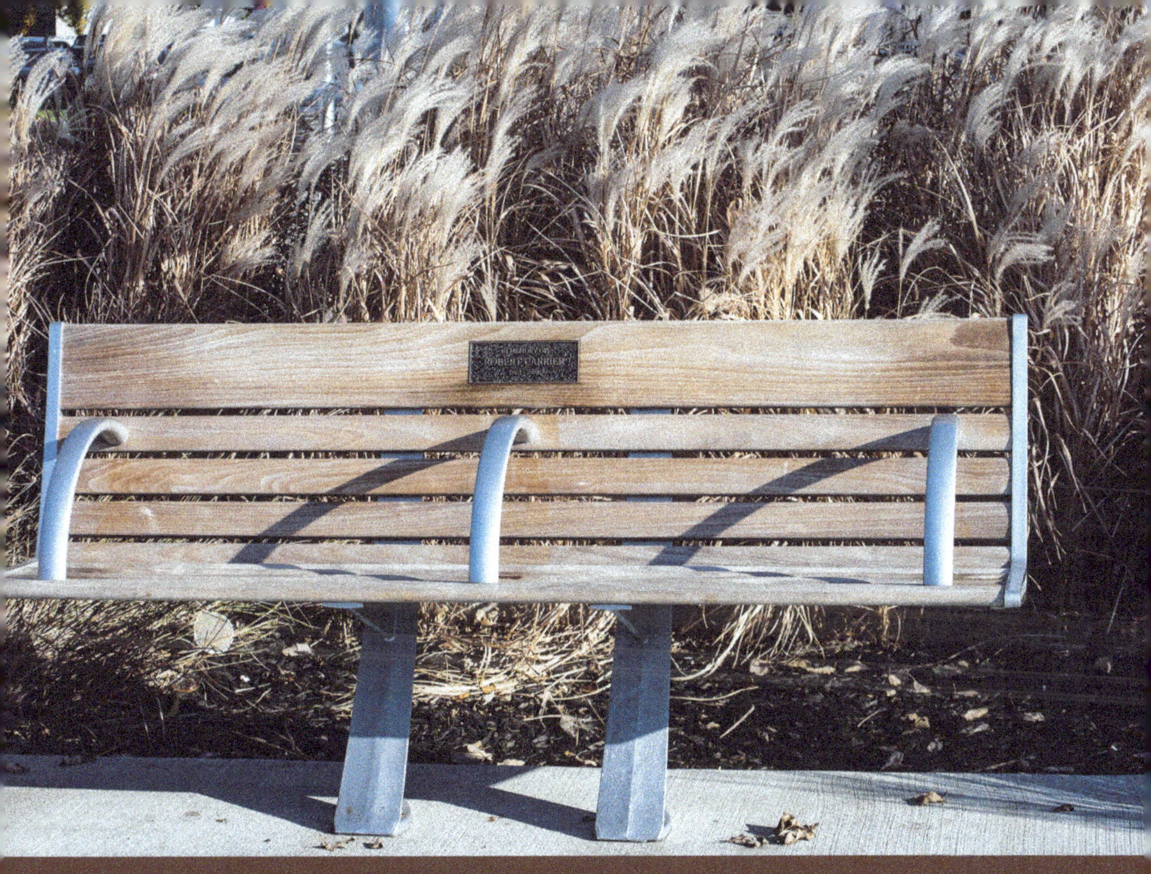

Bench was enjoying the respite, after a summer of offering comfort to people walking the waterfront. Though his back was to them, he could hear the grasses swishing the news that winter was coming. Cold never bothered him, and the grasses were good company.

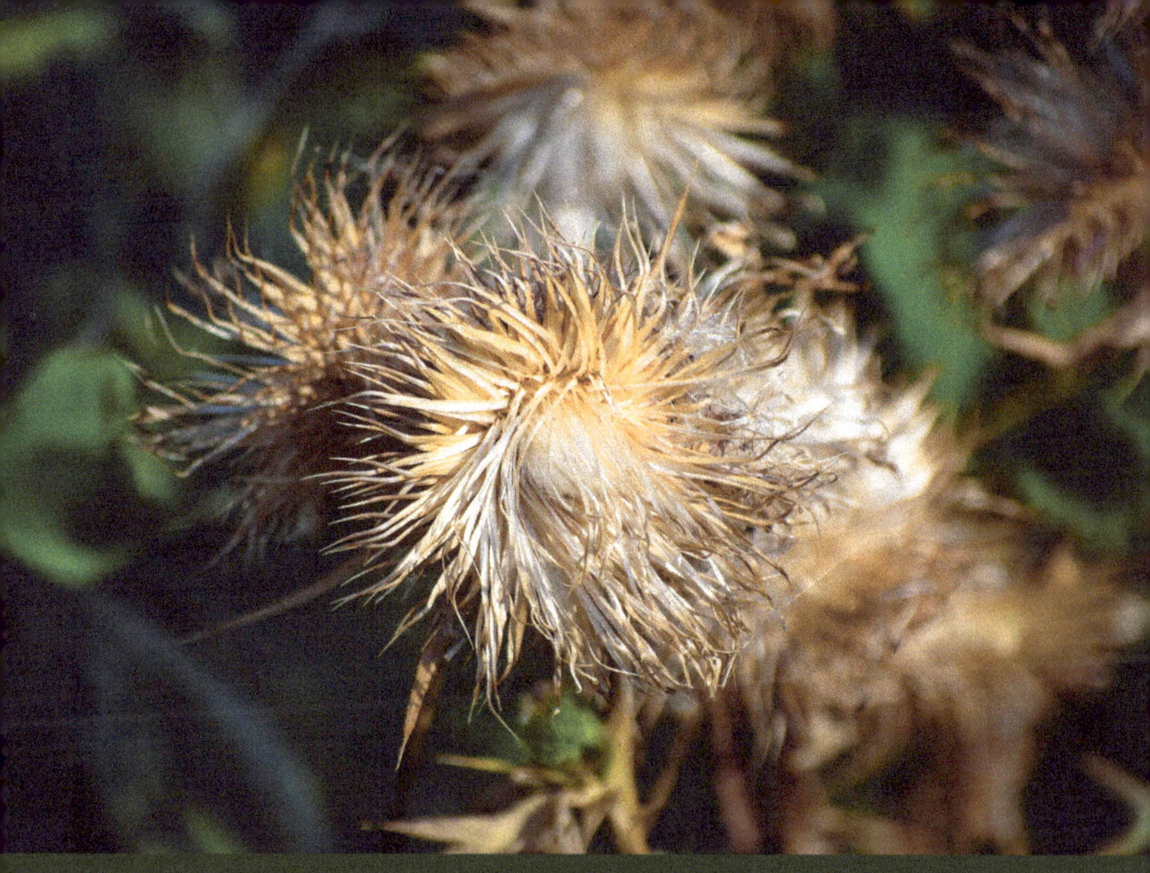

They danced in the sun, winked at the moon, and told bawdy stories. They were nearing their final flight. Freed of the constraints of their earlier days, they were not holding back. They had nibbled life. Now they were devouring it.

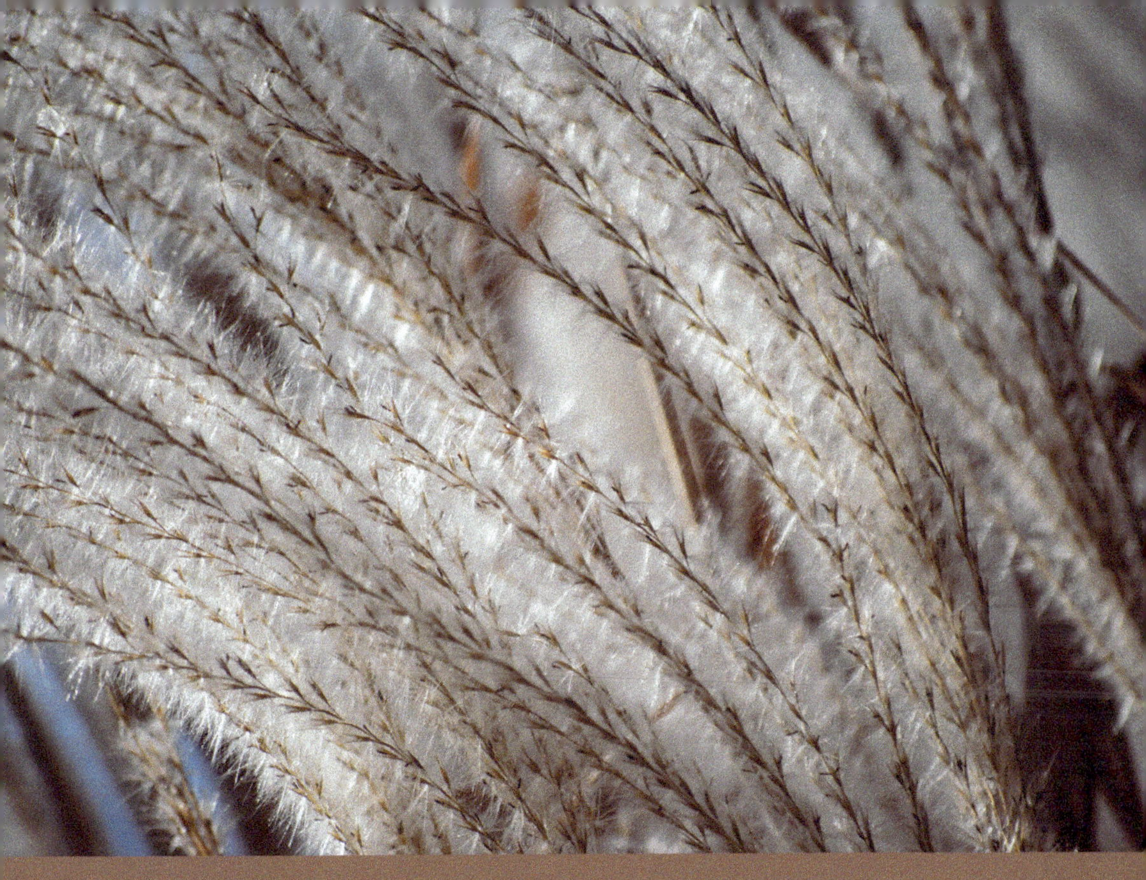

Unlike the seed pods that dropped by for visits, the grass seeds intended to stay home. They liked the stalks that held them. They had heard rumors that in spring People With Machines would cut them down. They intended to enjoy life until then.

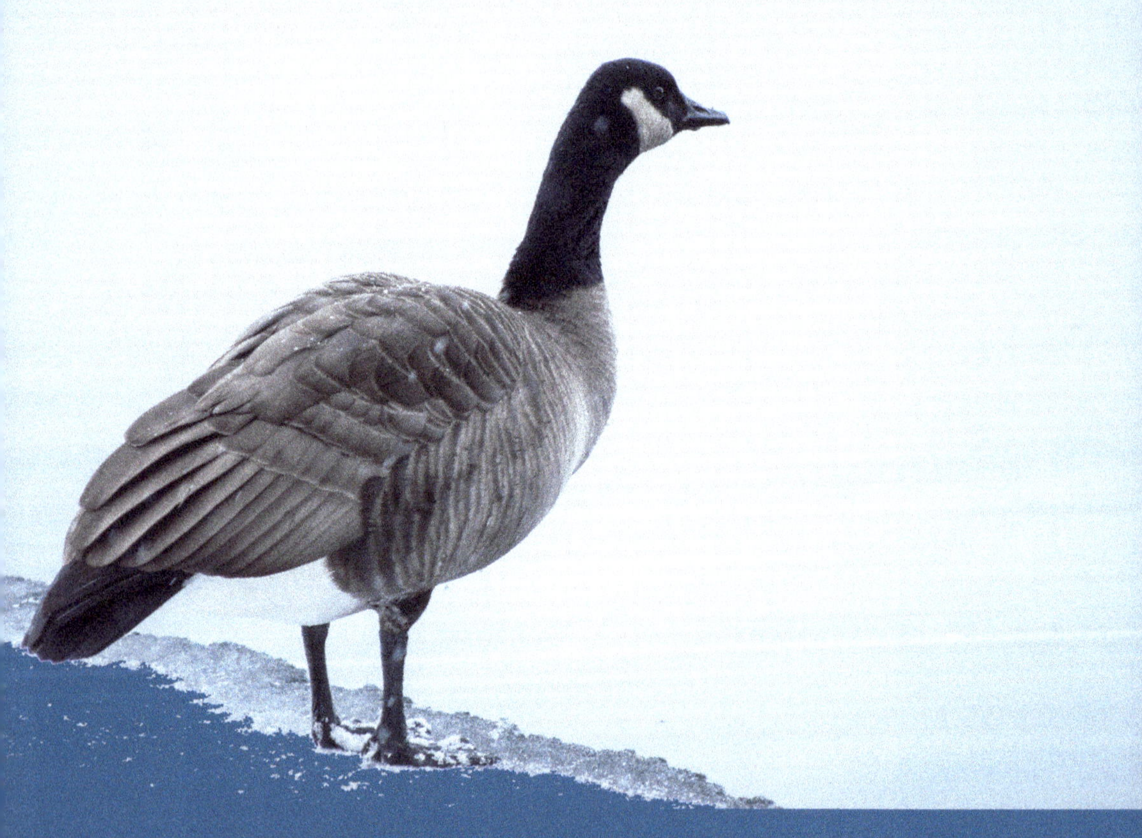

As snow fell softly, she stood at ice's edge and contemplated the unexpectedness of life. This was not how she envisioned "flying south" to end.

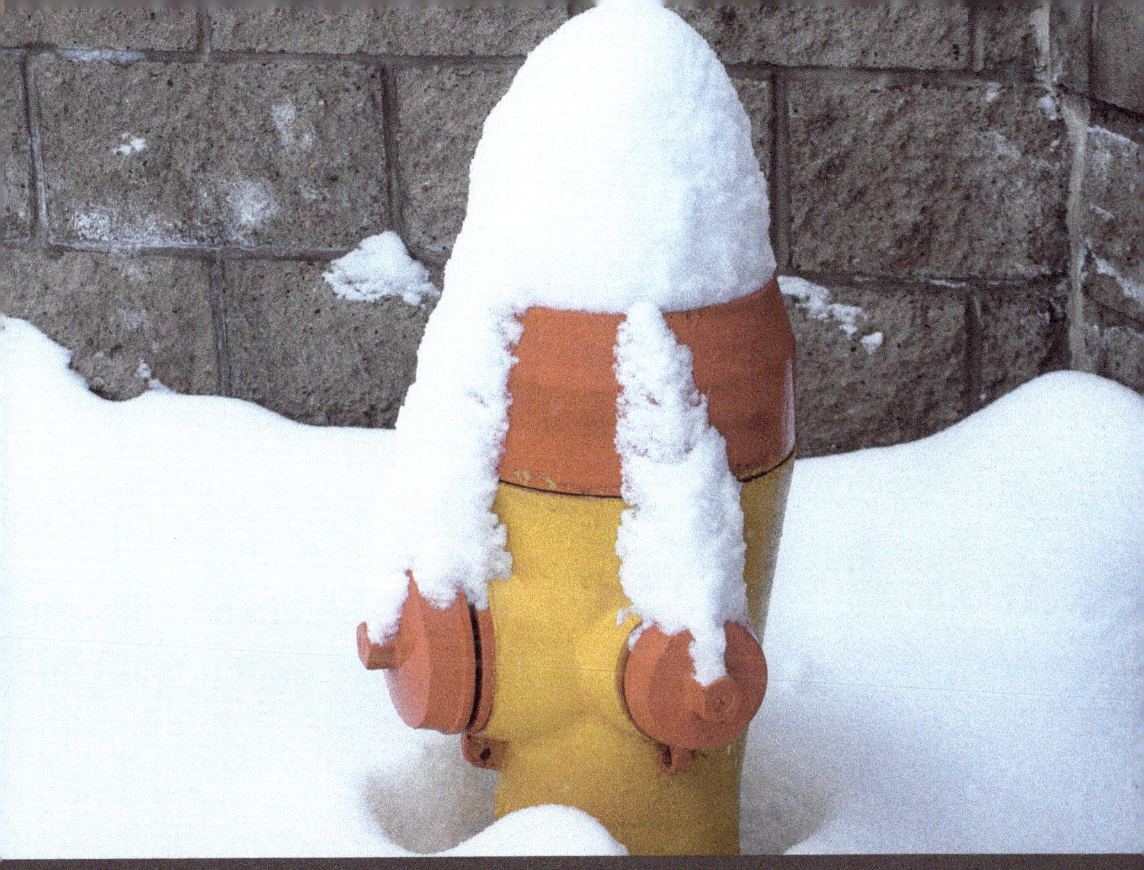

"Snow," said Hydrant. "You're getting closer, but you haven't quite given me the Roman helmet look. Thanks for trying."

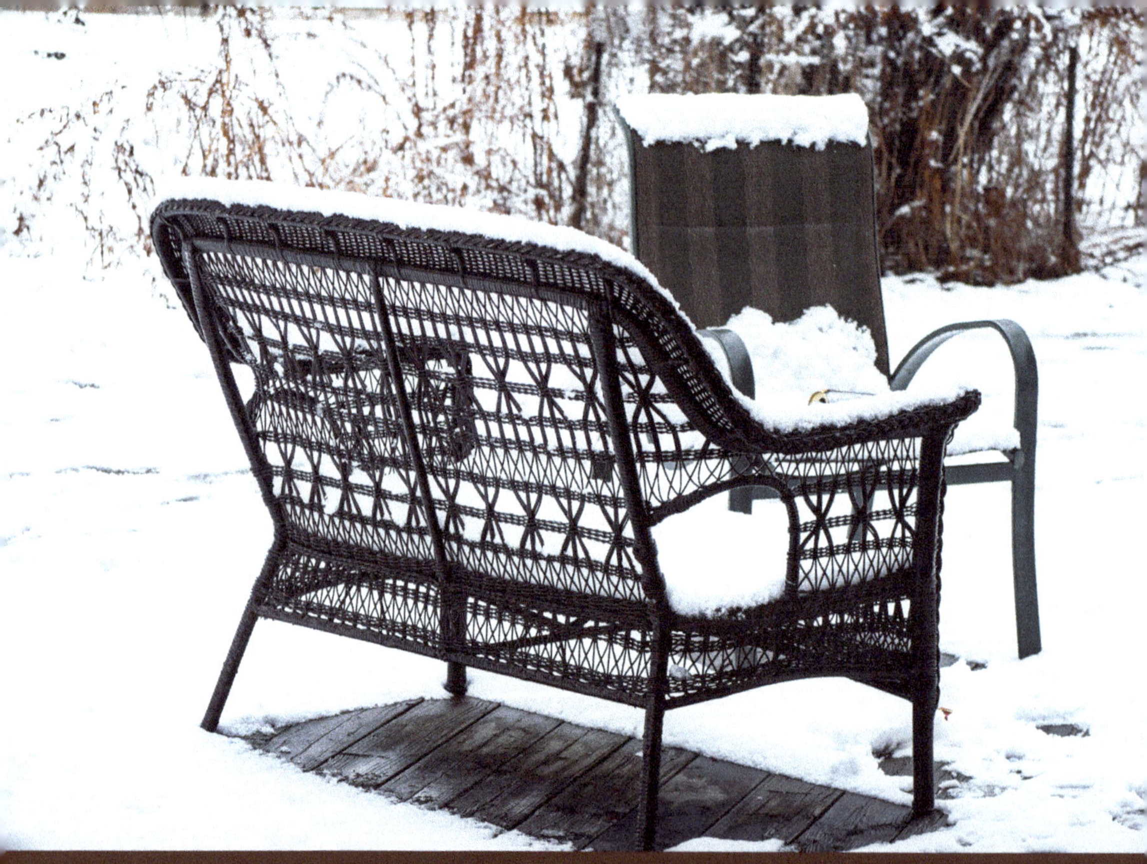

Only the night before, Chair and Loveseat had been sitting quietly on the patio of a townhouse. Then came The Night Guys, who moved them into the marsh. They knew their people would miss them, but they kind of liked the new scenery.

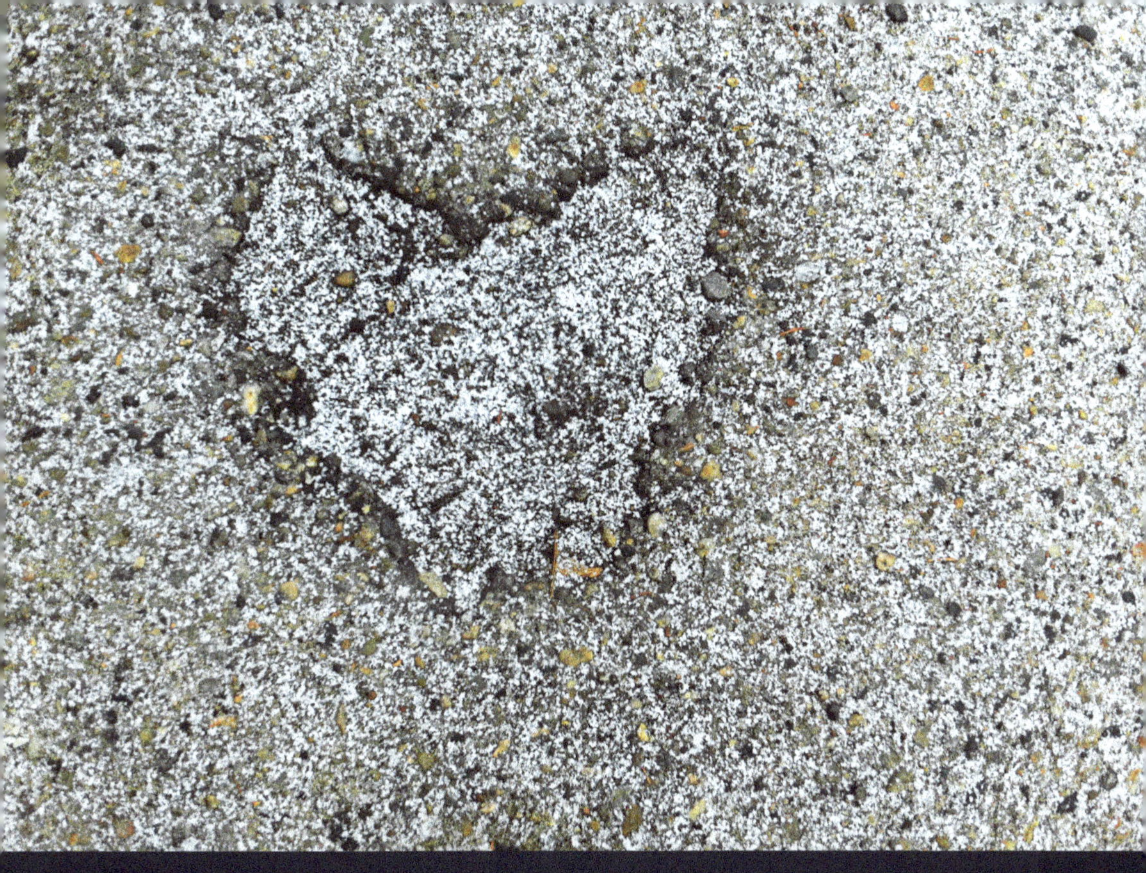

They paved over the grass to expand a parking lot, but all was not lost. Mother Nature knew how to crack open asphalt. The heart was her way of winking at the pavers and smiling at the sky.

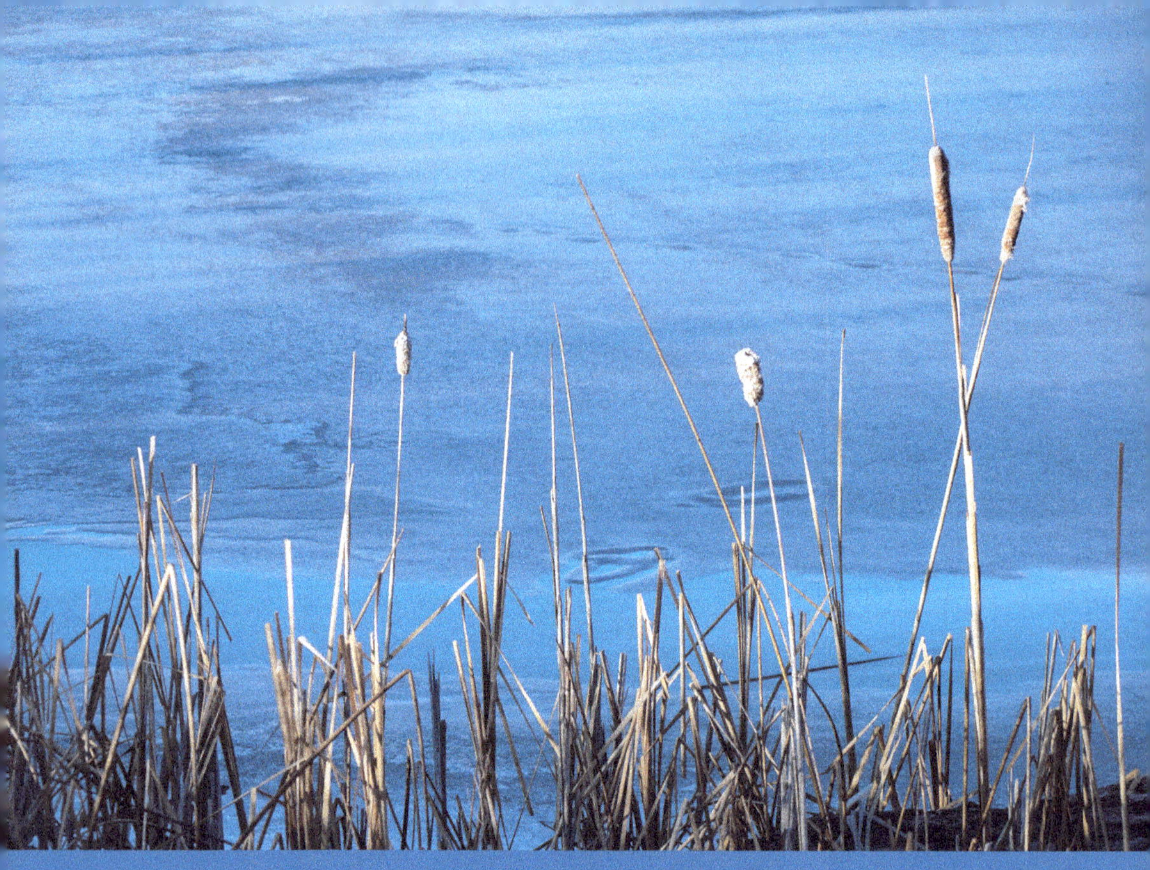

The reeds looked out at the ice. They missed their younger days. Then Sun emerged from behind the clouds. He bathed them with light and memories, of birds and fish they had met. They felt more ready for the transition ahead.

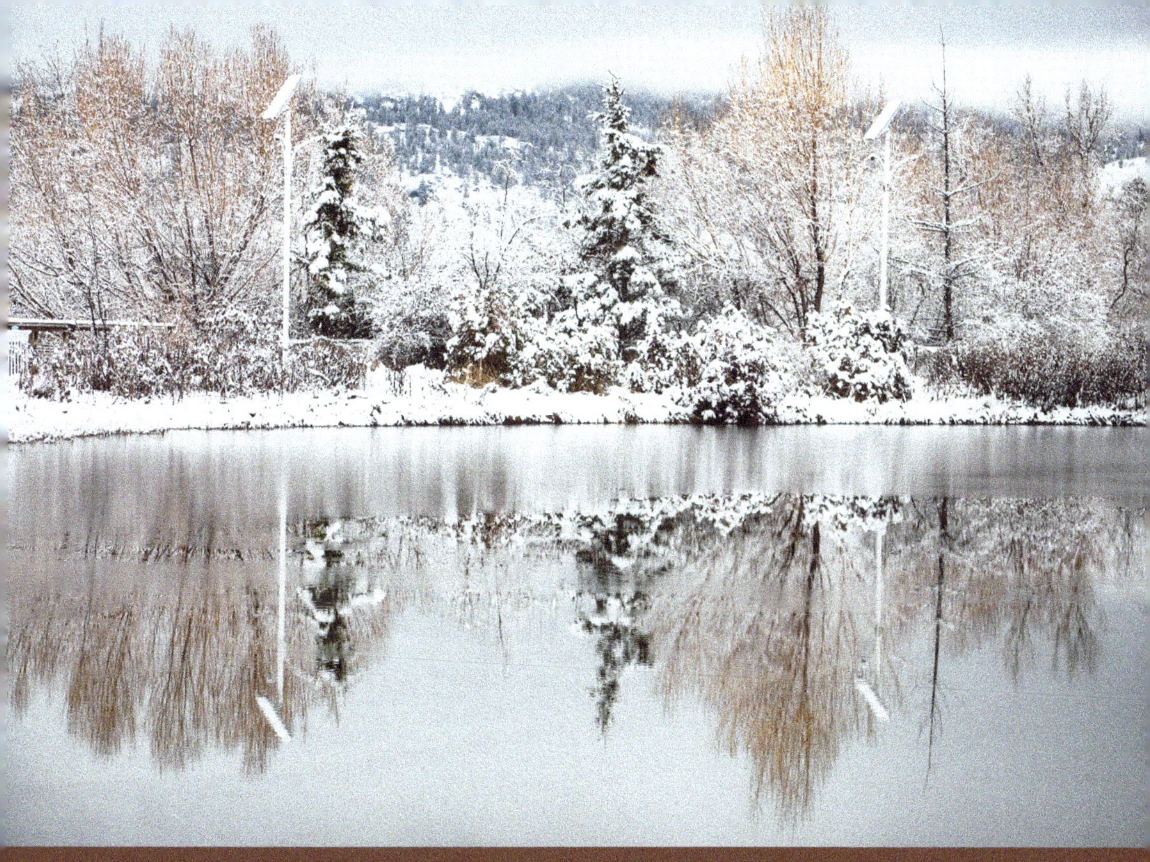

Year after year the solar lamps faithfully cast light when darkness fell. No one guessed their hearts were filled with longing for each other. Theirs was a love that would never be requited.

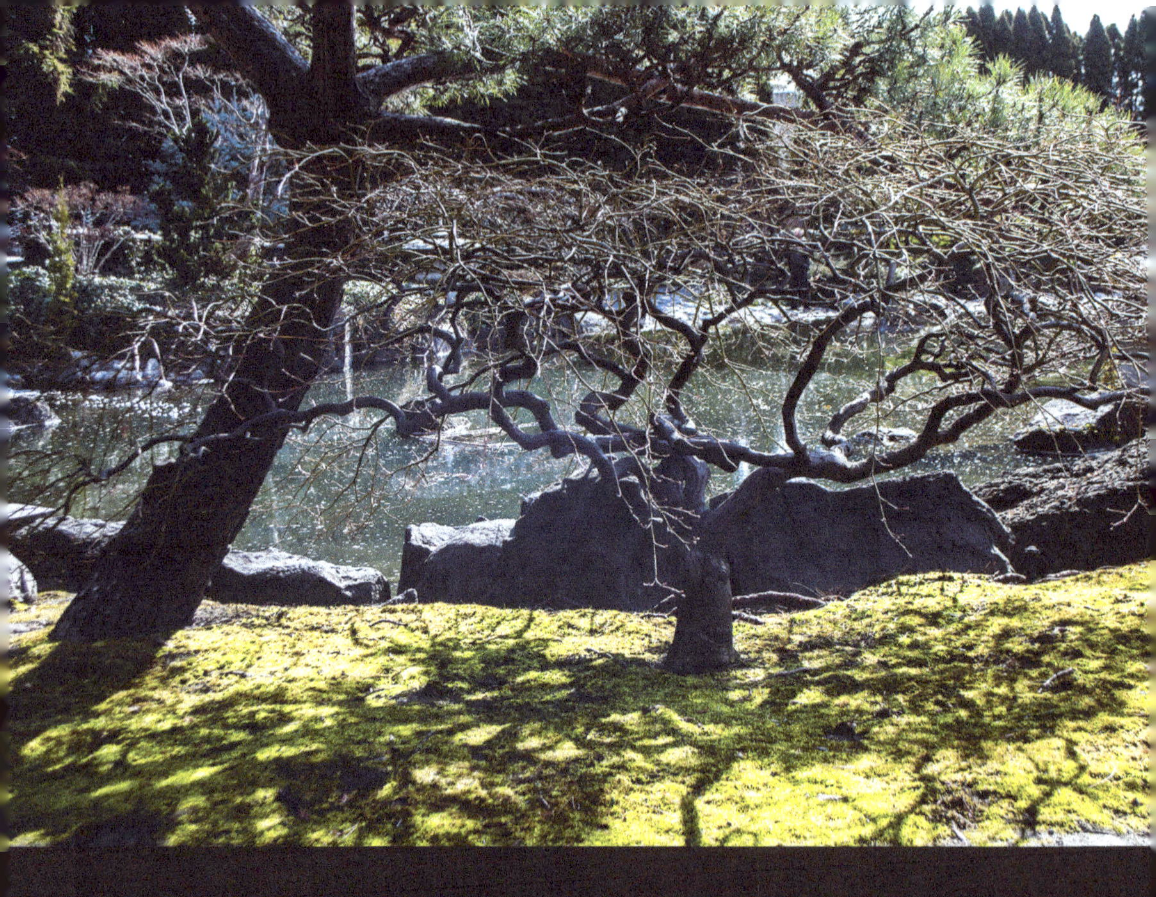

The Faerie Tree welcomed the longer days, after the cold grey of winter. Before long, she would be covered with leaves. On moonlit nights, tiny dancers would gather to move and sway beneath her branches.

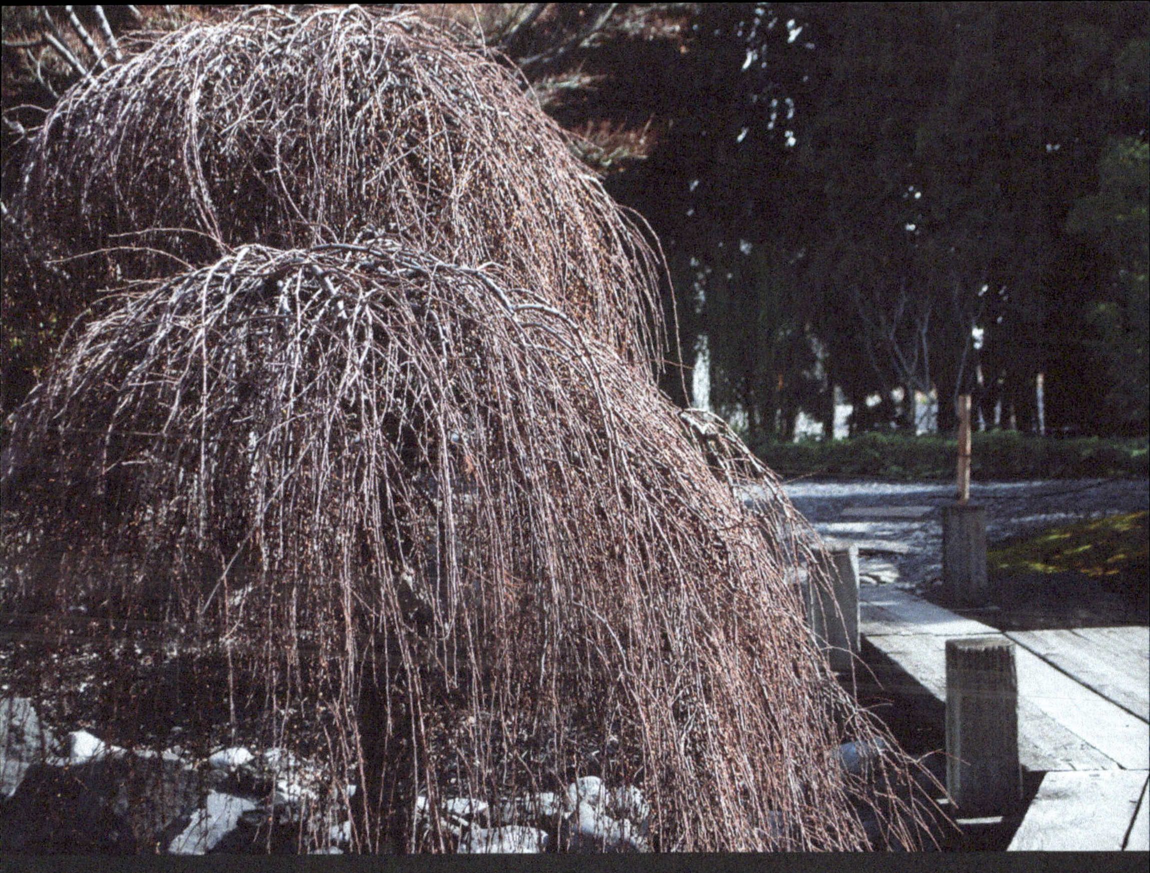

"You're looking a bit ragged," said Tall Tree. "You should talk," said Short Tree. "Birds can't even land on you, you're such a tangled mess." They both shook with laughter, remembering they had the same conversation every spring.

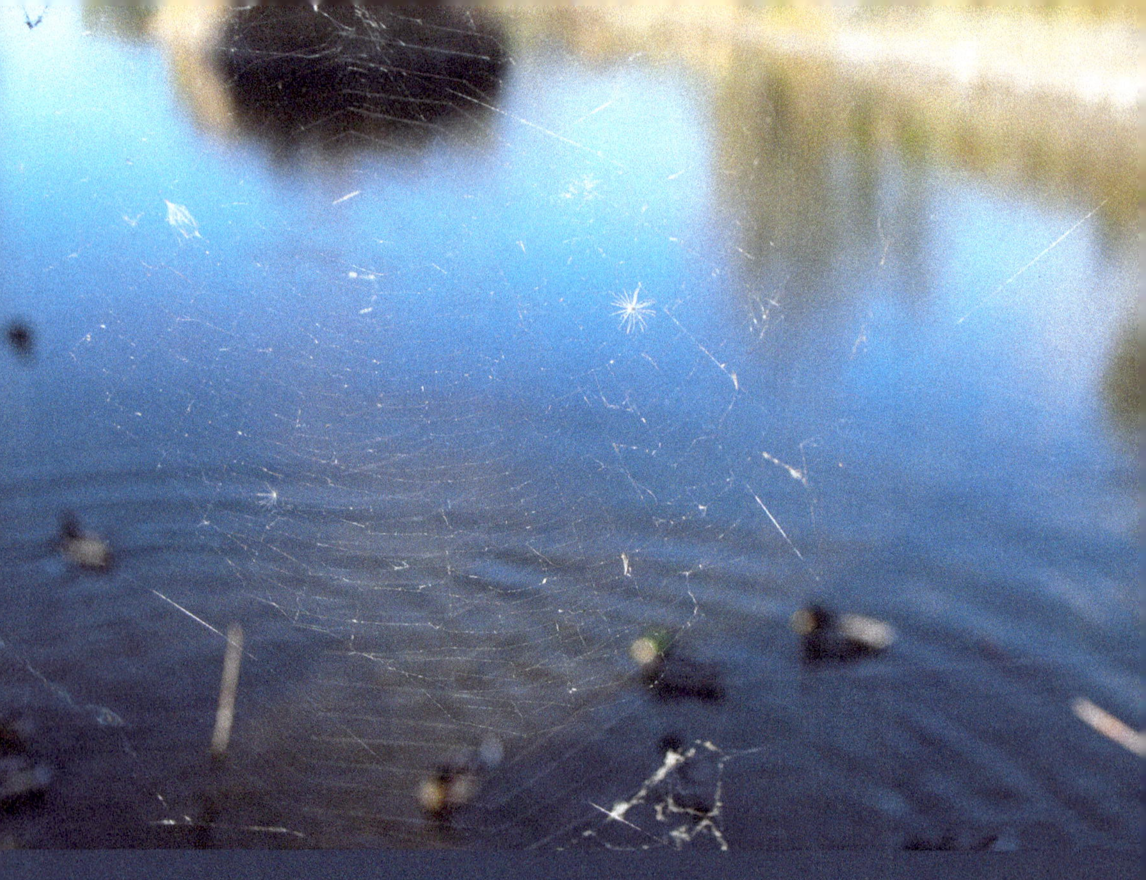

Elsa was disappointed. The spider next to her had dozens of flies in her web. Elsa had one. All she seemed to catch were bits of floating weeds. Elsa knew she created much prettier webs, but her neighbor had a better sense of where to spin them.

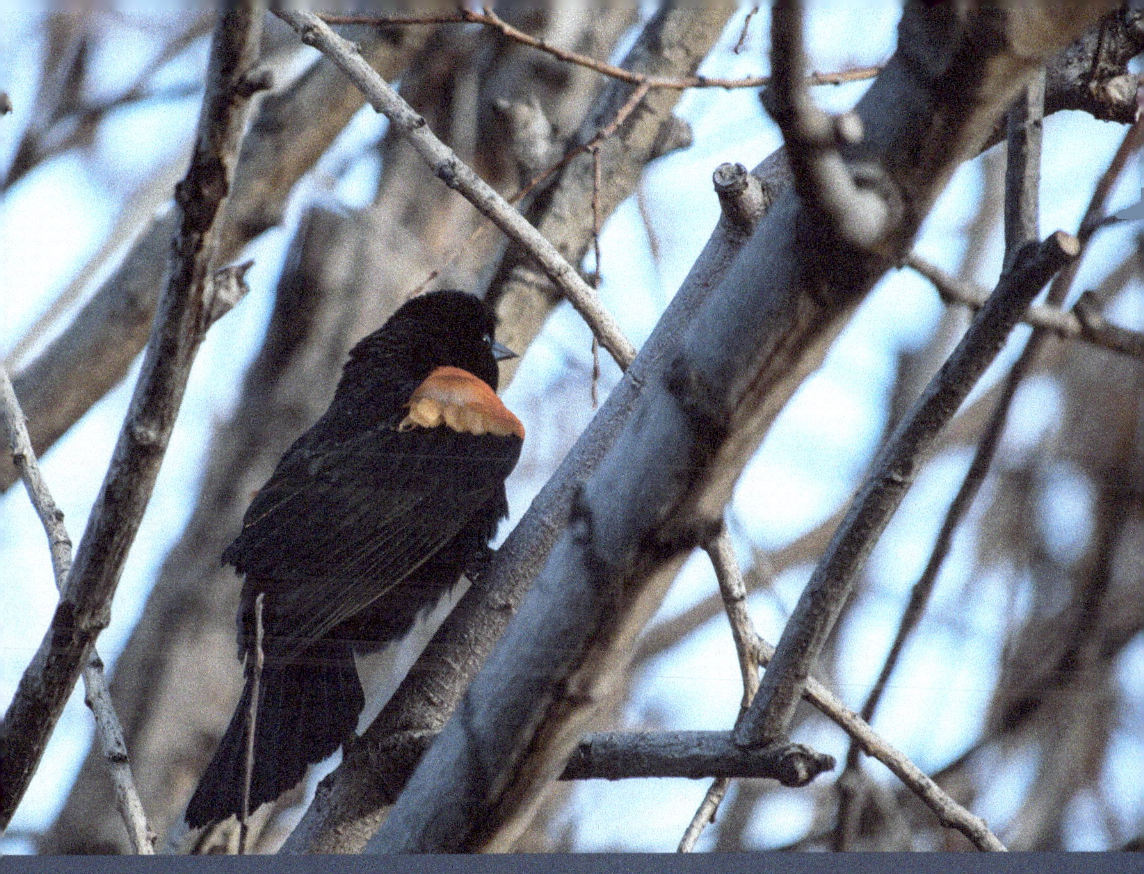

Scout was beginning to think Old Blackbird had been feeding him a line when he urged him to be the first bird to migrate back to the marsh. "You'll get first pick," he had said, but the promised bugs and greenery were in short supply.

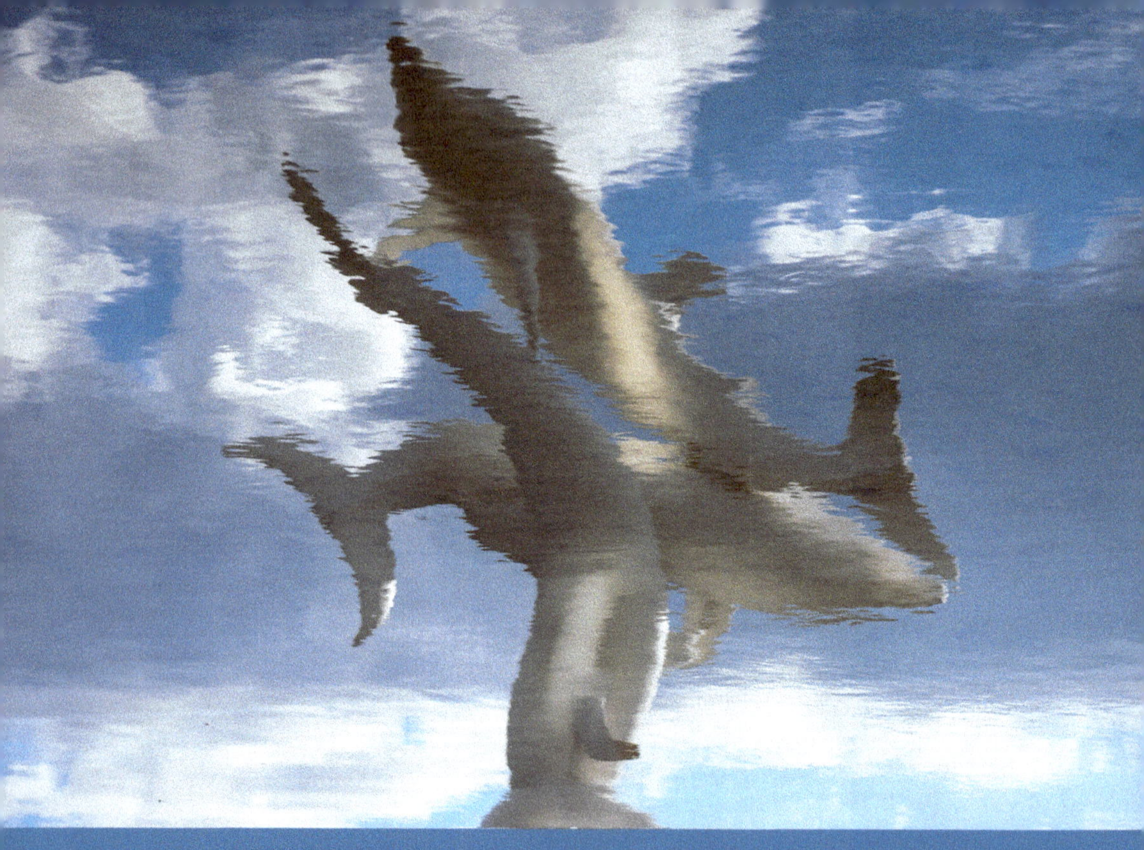

When light and wind were just right, Dolphins left the platform to which they were tightly secured and entered the realm of mystery. They swam with the clouds and dreamed of life untethered.

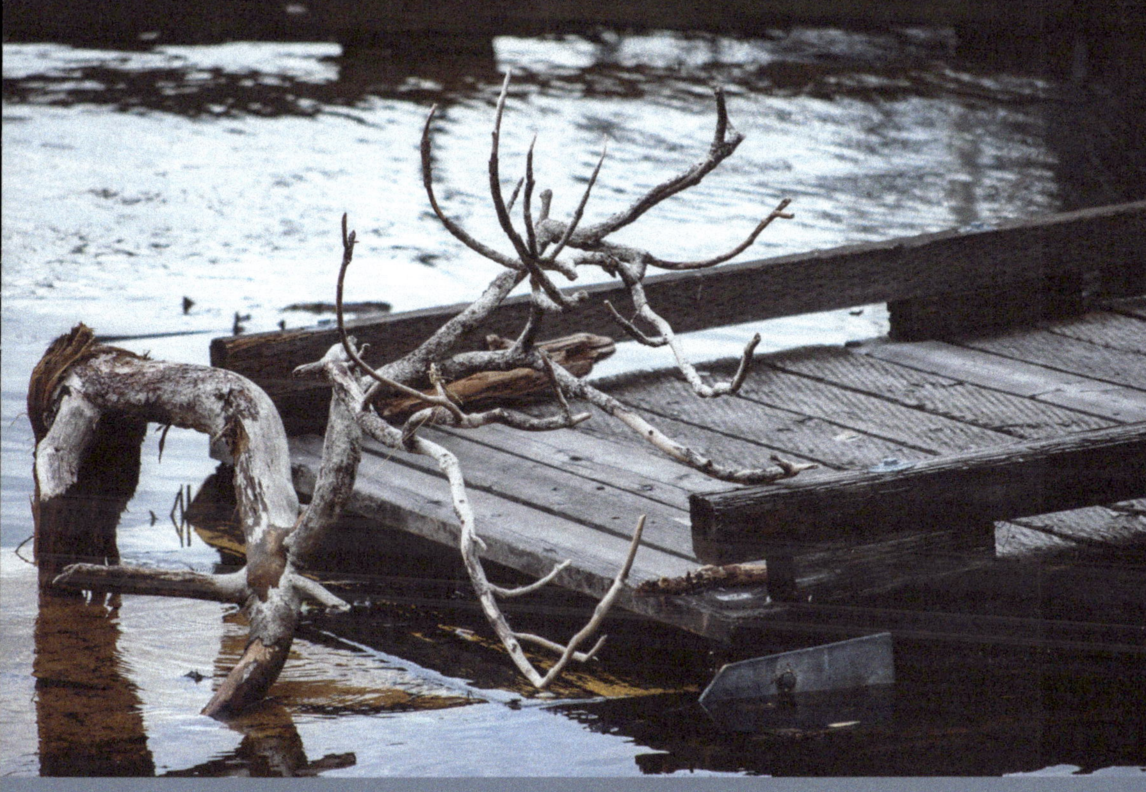

"So I was hanging around on a beach when Water swept me across the lake, and I ended up here." Dock was polite to the log but was a little tired of chatty newcomers washing up on him. He longed for normal water levels and summer boats.

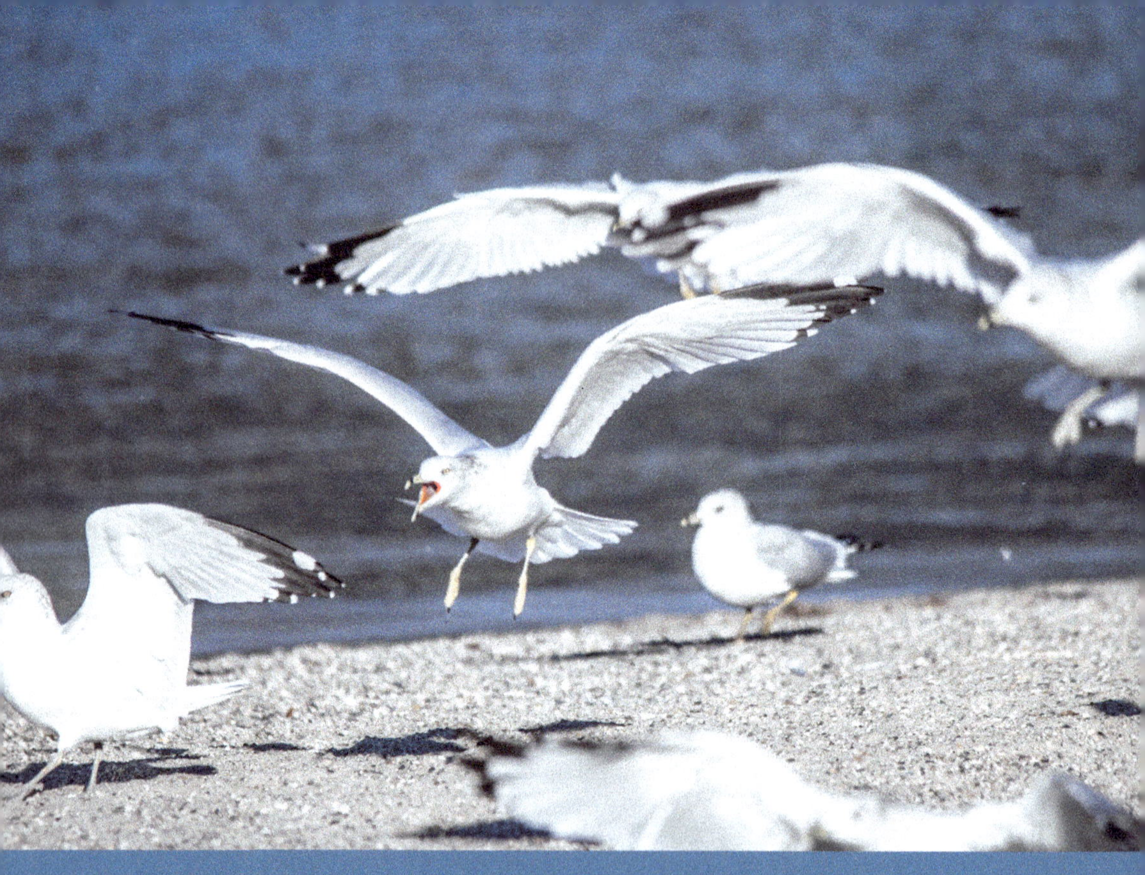

"Eagle! Eagle!" cried Jack. Even though the eagle was nowhere near, the trick worked every time. By the time the others settled, Jack had snatched the best bits of human food left on the beach.

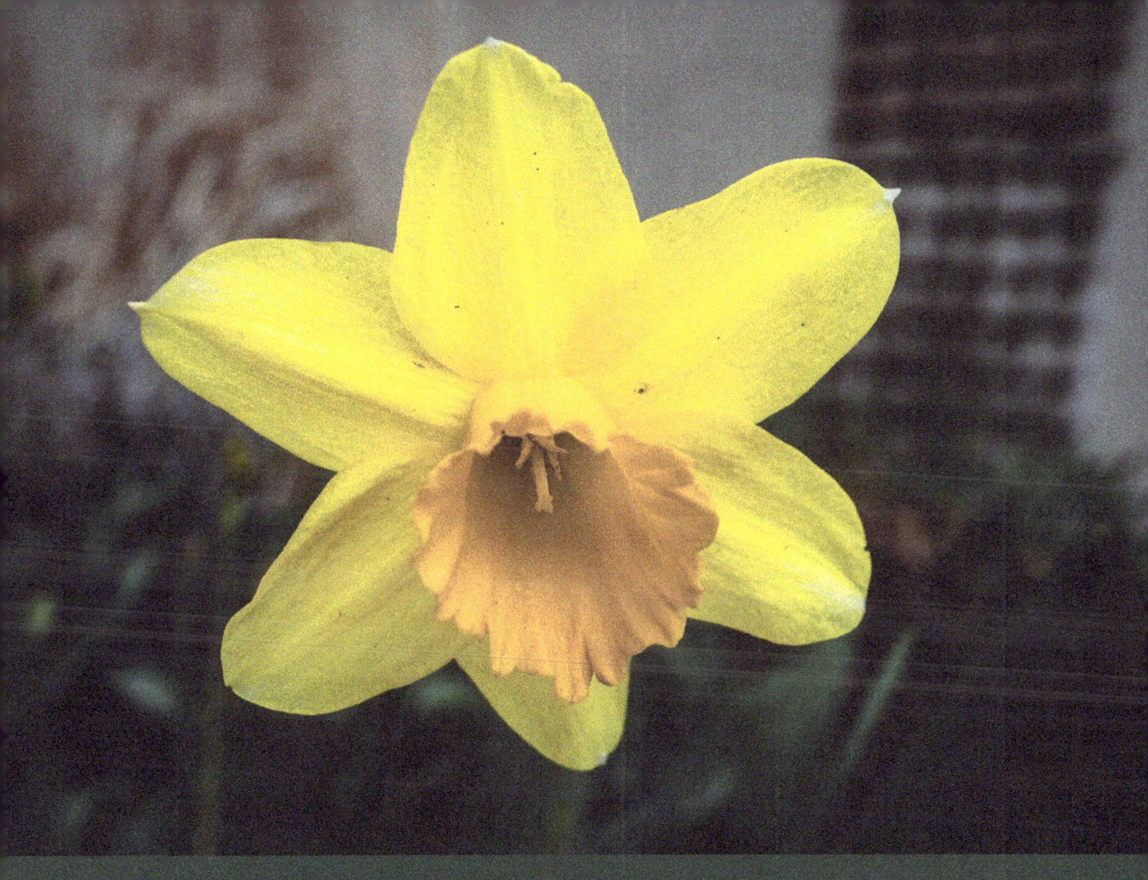

Daffodil opened her throat and sang lustily. She had
learned a lot of rude songs while she waited to bloom.
Worms knew dozens of them and depended on the
flowers to spread them around.

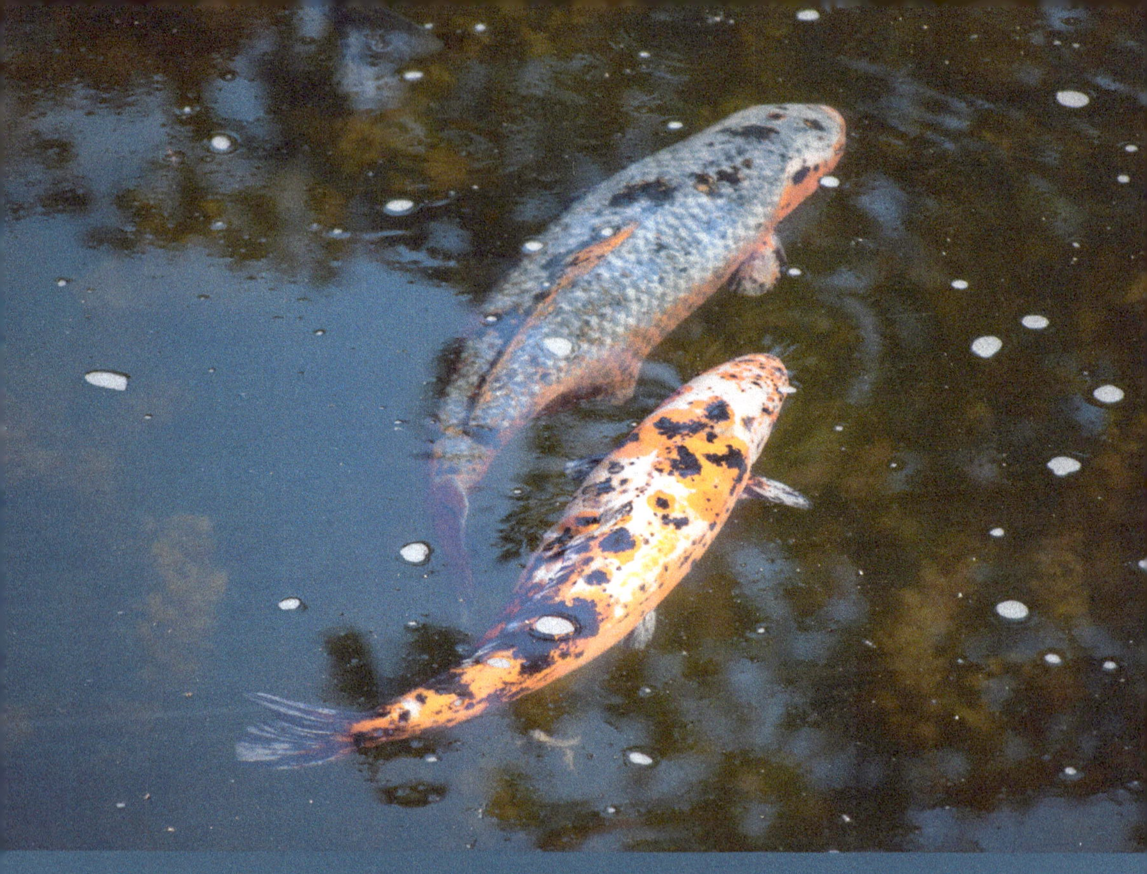

Stripe knew Spot admired him, but sometimes he wished the youngster would let him swim in peace.

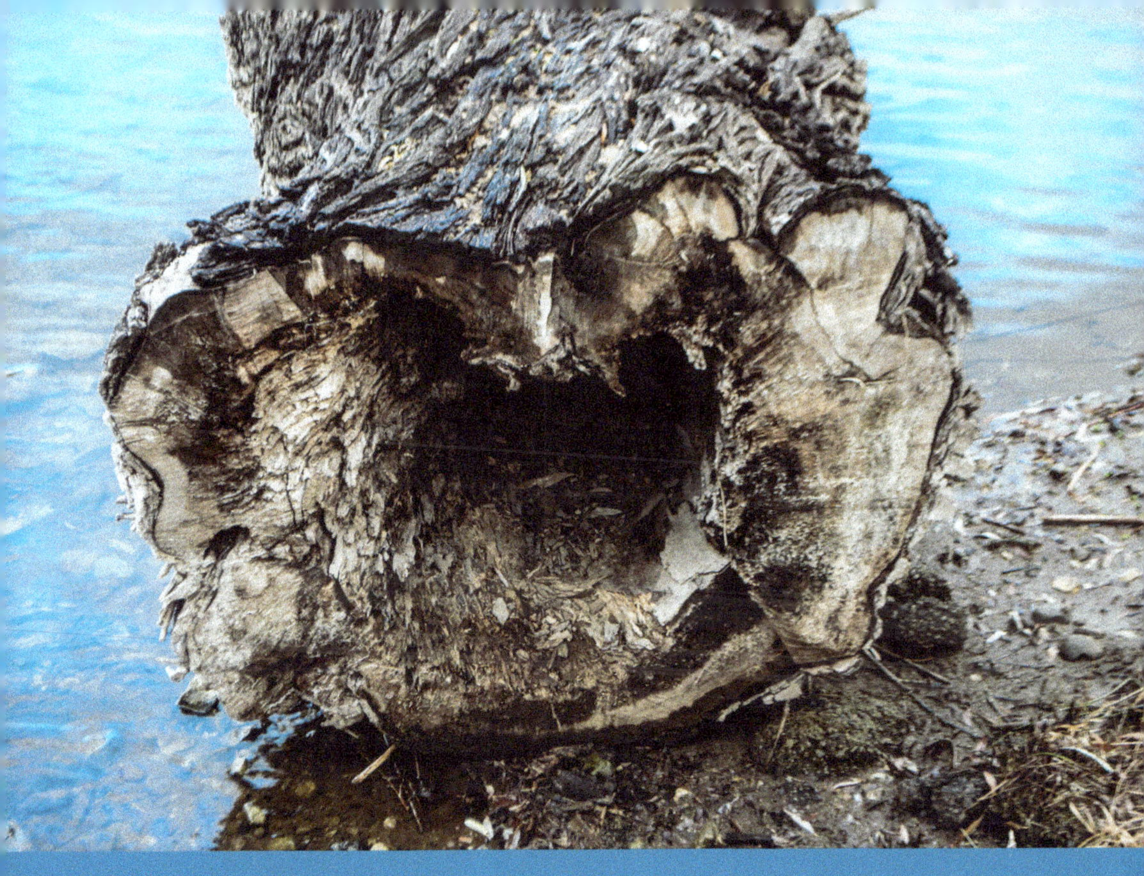

Log had seen a lot of the world since being cut from his roots. He had journeyed down rivers, across lakes, and into a marsh. When he came to rest in this strange place, he felt lonely and hollow. Then he realized the empty space was his open heart.

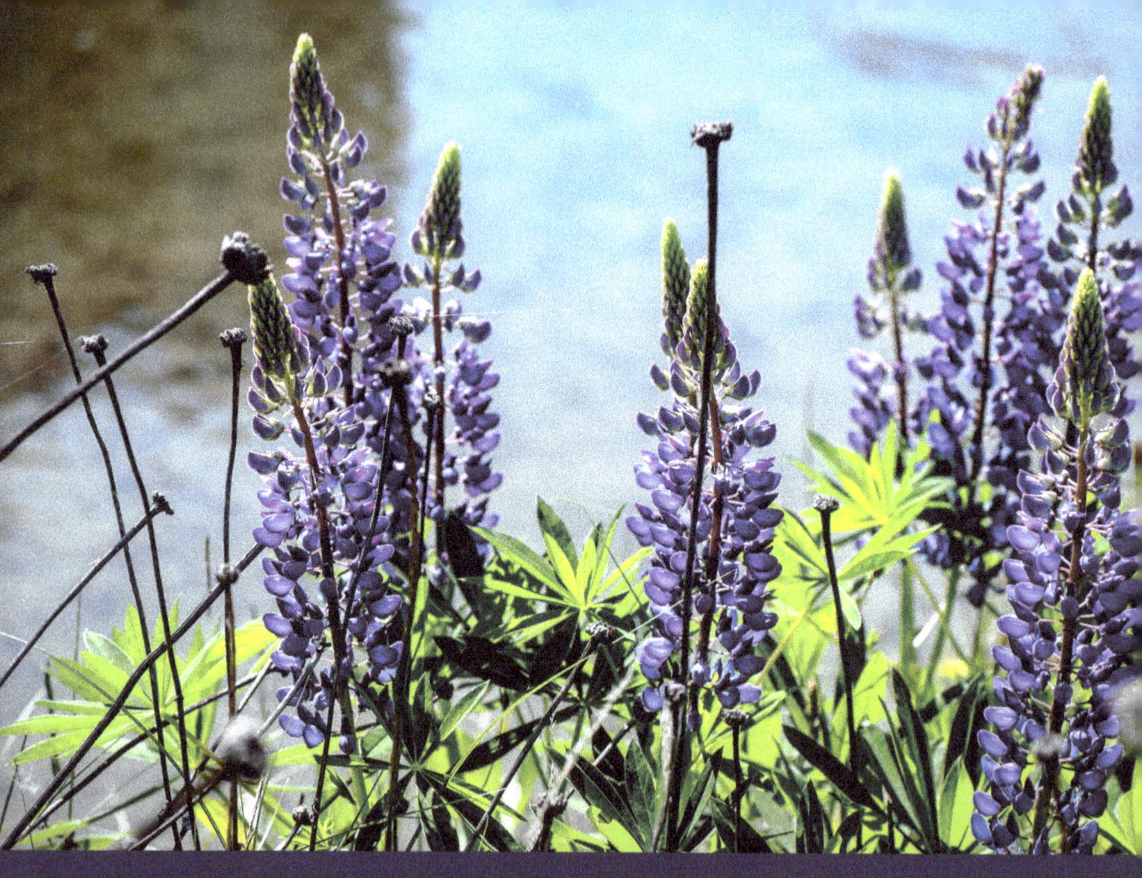

The spider was so tiny she escaped the notice of most predators. Her talent was her downfall. She was an exuberant spinner of exquisite web paths that sparkled in the sun and caught a bird's eye.

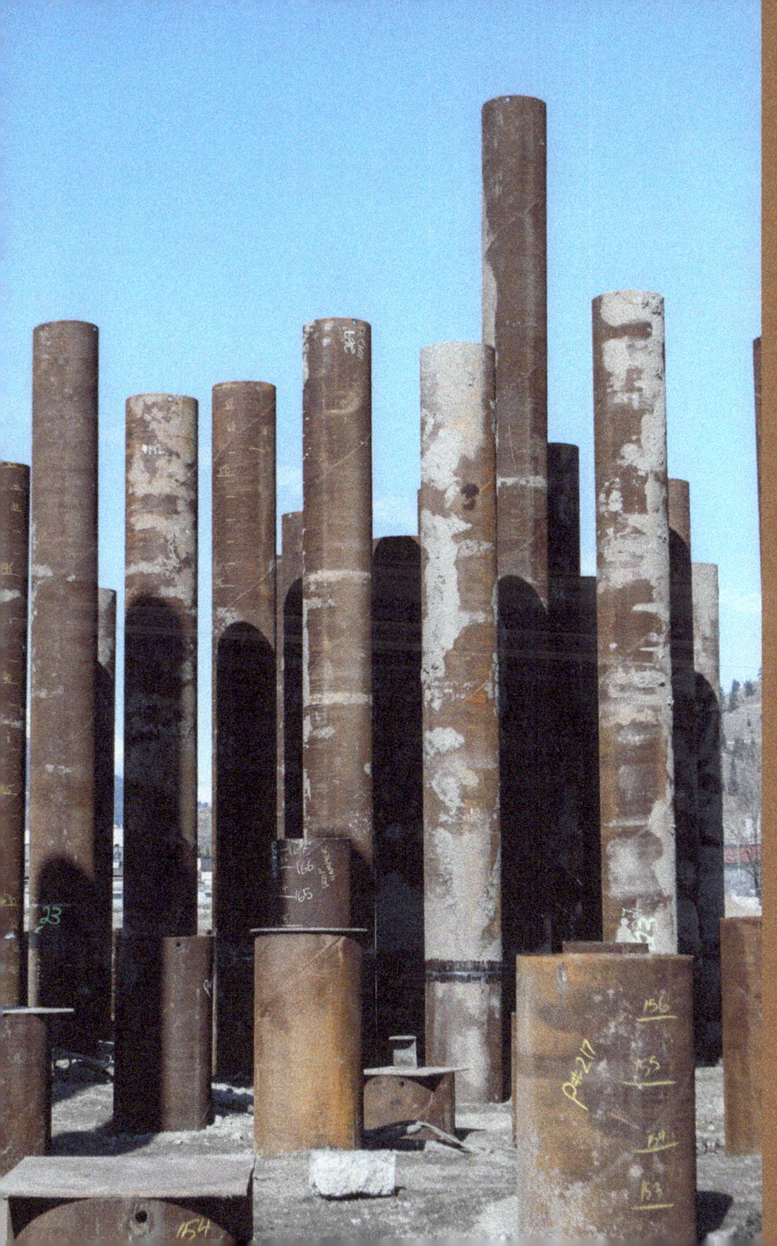

Now that some pipes were well above ground and others were nearly at earth level, they finally had a chorus full of harmonies. They worked out song arrangements so they could be ready to freak out the people who would buy the condos that would be built above them.

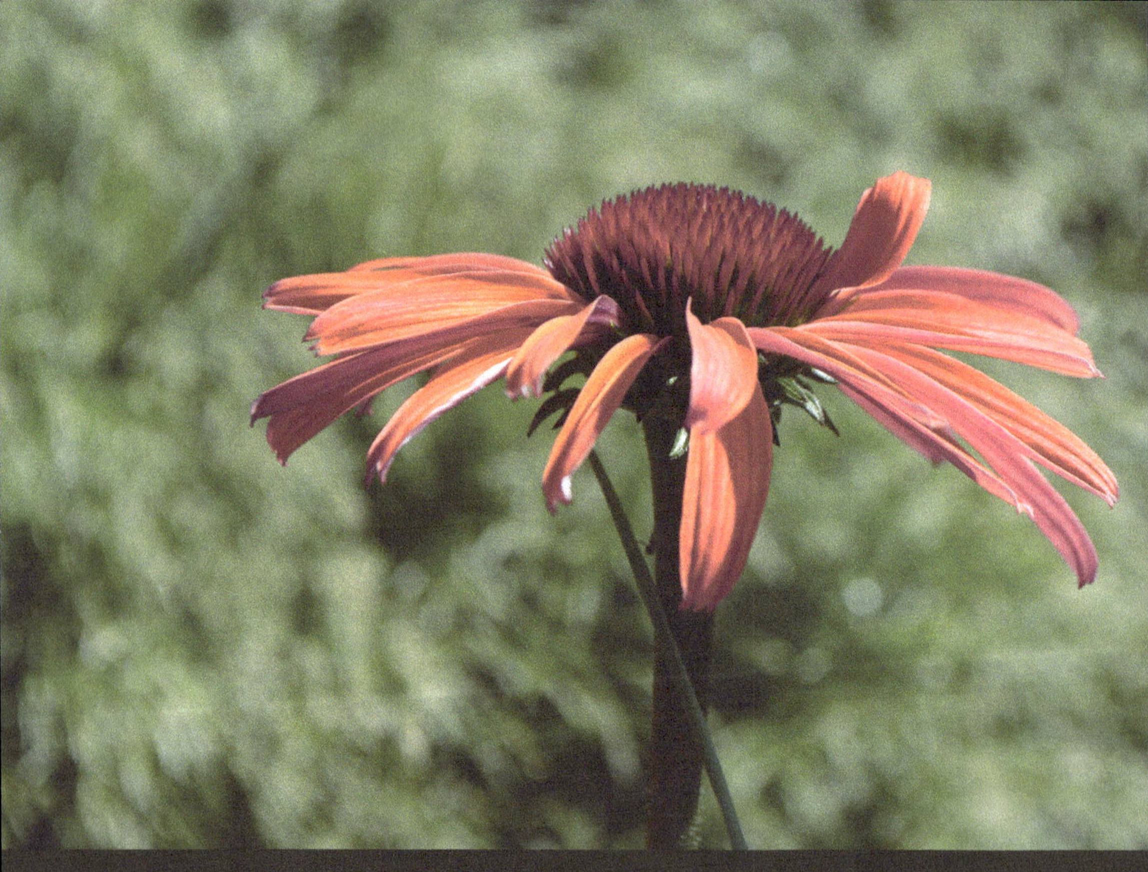

Coneflower lifted a petal to wave to her cousin in the next clump. It was a subtle gesture, visible only to her relative. She did not want to alarm the people who had stopped to admire her bright display.

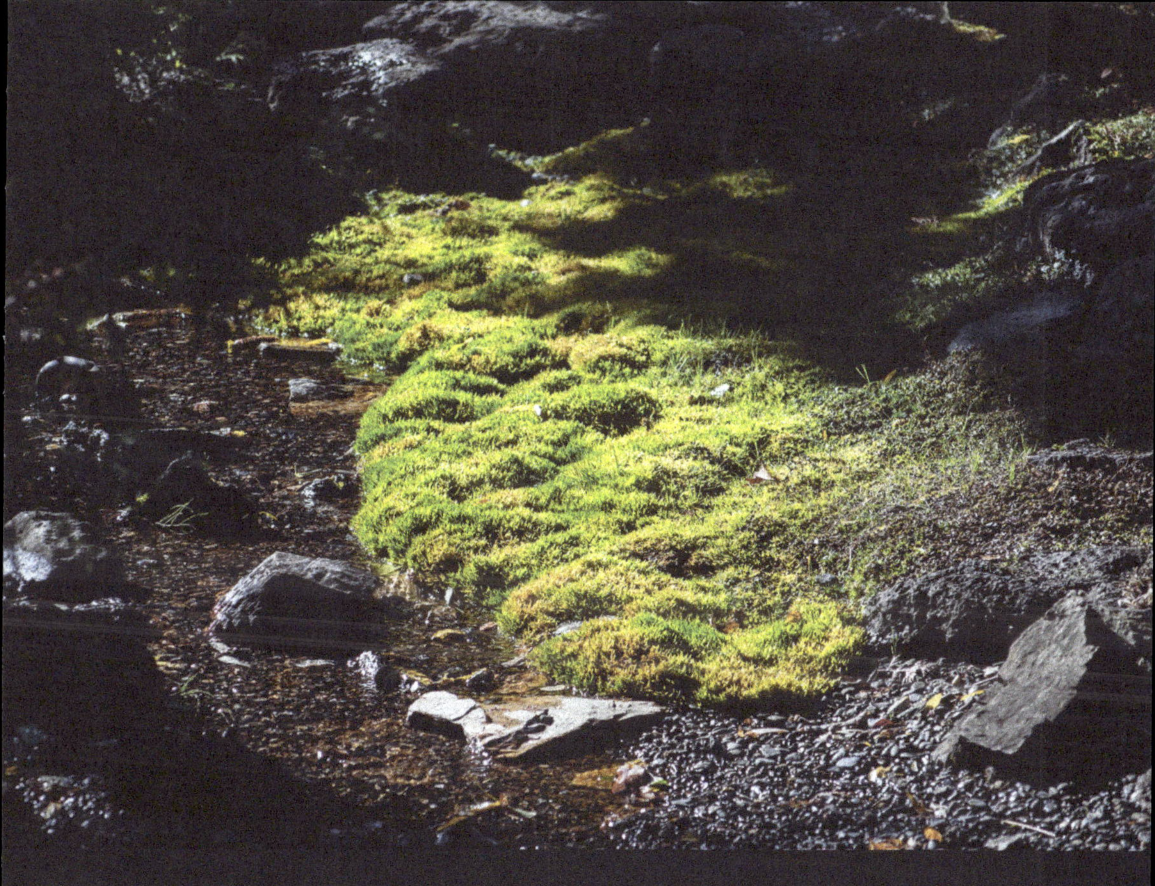

Moss made a soft bed to ease the stranger's sleep.
Rivulet moved quietly among the rocks, making a soft
sound to ease the stranger's troubles. The stranger had
never spent a night there, but Moss and Rivulet never
stopped preparing for him.

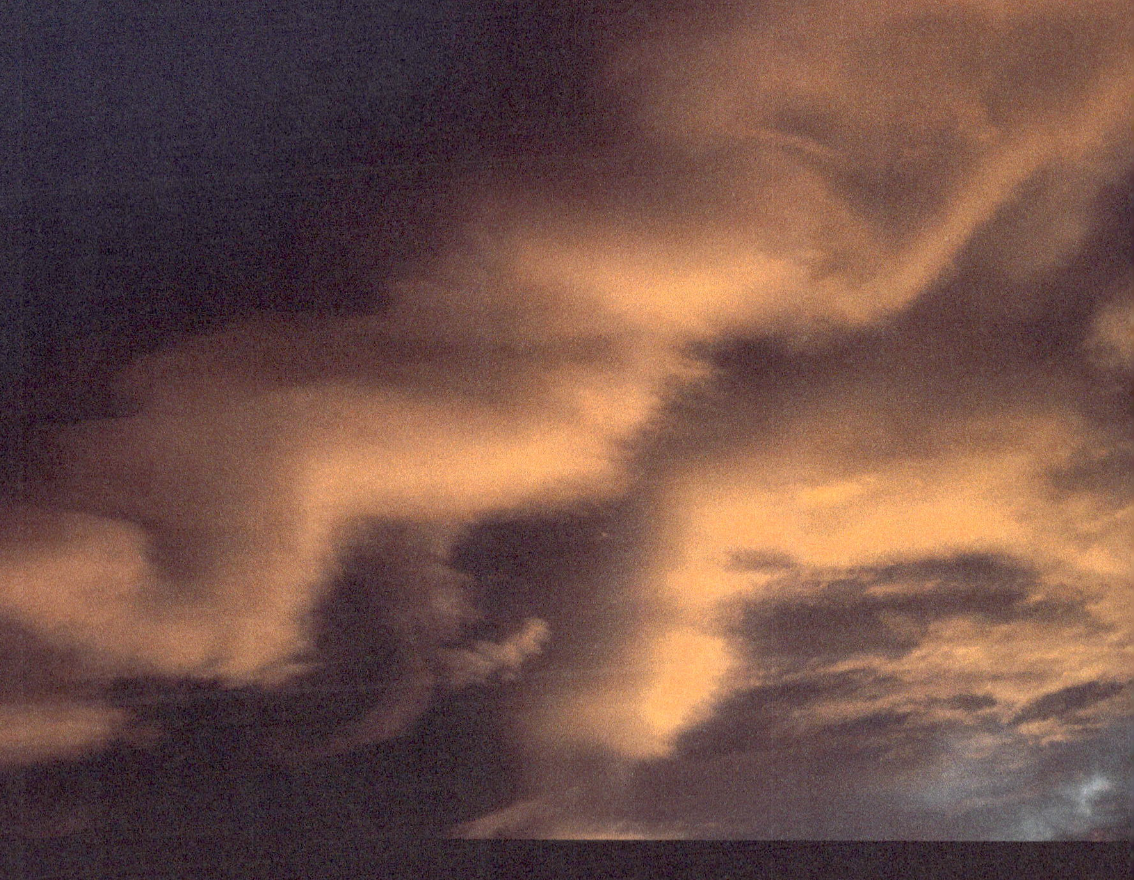

Sky had spent a long time planning this particular sunset. It had taken a lot of cooperation between clouds, wind and sun, but the result was worth every minute spent in preparation.

ABOUT THE AUTHOR

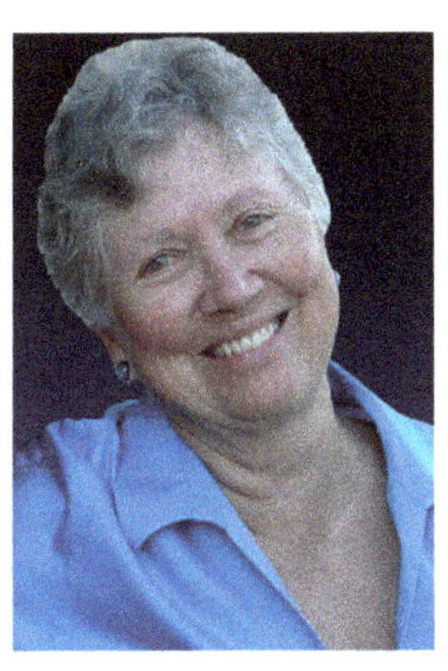

Cathryn Wellner is a writer, photographer and storyteller living in Kelowna, British Columbia, Canada. Her recent books include:

Small Scale Stories series (*That Tree Talked to Me, Parts of Me Are Still Amazing, The Disappearing Pumpkin Choir, In the Shelter of Each Other, Your Task Is to Be Admired, In the Country of Plastic, I'll Tell You a Story*)

Essay collections (*Hope Wins & Feisty Aging*)

In the Hug of Hills

Millie's Foster Family children's series (*Millie's Feathered Foster Family, Turkey Baby and the Hungry Hawk, Turkey Baby Finds Her Magic*)

You can find links to these and her other books at cathrynwellner.com. Contact her at cathryn@cathrynwellner.com or 778-478-2760. Her photographs can be found on her Web site, as well as on Facebook and Instagram.

BE A BOOK REVIEW ANGEL

If you enjoyed this book, please post a review on Amazon or Goodreads. Share it with friends and rave about it on social media. You can contact the author at cathryn@cathrynwellner.com.

Authors rely on their readers to help spread the word about books they like. People who review books are special kinds of reader angels. I guarantee when you review this book, or any other book that has given you pleasure in any way, you'll feel those wings poking out your back. Look closely in the mirror, and you might even see a halo.